John Bull Smith Dimitry

Lessons in the history of Louisiana

From its earliest settlement to the close of the civil war

John Bull Smith Dimitry

Lessons in the history of Louisiana
From its earliest settlement to the close of the civil war

ISBN/EAN: 9783337222567

Printed in Europe, USA, Canada, Australia, Japan

Cover: Foto ©ninafisch / pixelio.de

More available books at **www.hansebooks.com**

LESSONS

IN THE

HISTORY OF LOUISIANA,

FROM

ITS EARLIEST SETTLEMENT TO THE CLOSE OF THE CIVIL WAR,

TO WHICH ARE APPENDED

LESSONS IN ITS GEOGRAPHY AND PRODUCTS.

BY
JOHN DIMITRY, A. M.

A. S. BARNES & COMPANY.
NEW YORK, CHICAGO AND NEW ORLEANS.
1877.

PREFACE.

YOUTHS' Histories of the United States are not wanting. They crowd our schools, and are the despair of our booksellers. But there is a clearly defined want of the day, which is only now being partially filled. The growing pride of the individual States calls for a record of the names and of the events, of which each may have reason to be proud. Able writers have, for a long time, systematically ignored this call. For a State history, they have continued to give a history of the United States. But the States have been gradually awakening to a sense of their needs. New York and Virginia, South Carolina and Massachusetts, Georgia and Rhode Island, Connecticut and Maryland, have had their Colonial chronicles embalmed in the big histories of the Continent, to be read and re-read by the children of the whole country. Nor is there anything strange in this. These Colonies had autonomy before the Articles of Confederation had been accepted, or the Federal Constitution had been ratified. Without them, the first rosy dawnings of American History would have been night—not day.

But Louisiana, like other States formed since the organization of the Federal Government, has been utterly neglected in this direction. She has had able histories for grown-up people ; but none for children—plenty of strong meat for men, but no milk for her babes.

What the author has aimed at has been:

1. To teach the boys and girls of Louisiana, for the first time, that they have a history of théir own, of which they may be proud—a history every bit as authentic and valuable as the annals of Puritan Massachusetts or Catholic Maryland.

2. To explain to them that special mystery of the history of their State—the rearing of her colonial structure by one nation, and its blending into a colonial dependence on another.

Every average child has something to say about the change of Dutch New Amsterdam into English New York. But what does he know of the transfer of his own State from French Bienville to Spanish O'Reilly? Or from Spanish Salcedo to French Laussat back again? Or from French Laussat to American Claiborne?

3. To make them familiar with the physical configuration of Louisiana, which is, in itself, too peculiar to be properly understood, as taught in our great Geographies, scattered broadcast in our schools, both public and private, of this country.

The author has adopted what, he believes, has been called, with a ponderous grace, the "catechetical plan." He is fully aware that, in the minds of the newest bookmen of the day, there is a certain prejudice against the system. He is no convert to such a prejudice. The great fault, he conceives, of most of the histories of the day for children—whether catechetical or continuous—has been that the writers have chosen to appeal to the reason alone, instead of to a fair mingling of reason and fancy in the mind of the young student—in other words, to use the cold chisel of the sculptor, rather than the warm brush of the painter. The Socratic method of the old classic days brought out the real culture of the Athenian man. The Socratic method in history brings out the real interest of the American child.

He might claim as a novelty in this class of works, the prominence given to the Geography of the State, and to the productions of her soil. The Divisions marked "Geography" and "Products"—if not complete in themselves—give information not afforded in any text-book.

The author ventures here to call attention to a certain feature of his work. What he has written is the history of a Southern State, by a Southern man. It is not wise, in any sense, to reopen wounds now healing over. In treating of the events of the Civil War upon the territory of Louisiana, he has tried to give the facts without throwing a slur upon any of the actors. It is right that the sons and daughters of a great State should know what has taken place upon the soil of their common Mother. It would be wrong if they should—from the record made by him—learn to think unjustly of those who were participants, either friends or foes. To the author—a firm and honest believer in reconciliation between North and South—the restored Union means peace and prosperity to Louisiana, as to her sister Southern States.

In this little book, he is unwilling to teach any other lesson.

J. D.

Note.—I desire, here, to return my sincere acknowledgments to my friend, Major William M. Robinson, for his kindness in placing at my disposal, the treasures of his Louisiana Library. For myself, student as well as compiler, those treasures have proved invaluable.

TABLE OF CONTENTS.

PART I. HISTORY.

10 *CONTENTS.*

PART II. GEOGRAPHY.

PART III. PRODUCTS.

INTRODUCTION.

QUESTION. *What is Louisiana?*

ANSWER. Louisiana is one of the sovereign States, forming the Republic of the United States.

To what section of the United States does Louisiana belong?

After whom was Louisiana named?

Louis the Fourteenth, King of France.

Why was it named after that King?

Because it was during his reign that its territory was first discovered by the French explorer, La Salle, in 1682.

What is the capital of Louisiana?

New Orleans.

What was the population of the State at the last U. S. census?

In 1870, its population was 726,276.

What can you say of its government?

It is popular and elective.

Into how many great branches is the government divided?

Into four branches.

How are these known?

As the Executive, Legislative and Judiciary Depart ments, and the Department of Public Education.

Of whom does the Executive Department consist?

A Governor, Lieutenant-Governor, a Secretary of State, an Attorney General, a State Auditor, and a State Treasurer.

What constitutes the Legislative Department?

A General Assembly, comprising a Senate and a House of Representatives.

Of what is the Judiciary Department composed?

A Supreme Court consisting of one Chief Justice and four Associate Judges, together with inferior Courts.

Who is the chief of the Department of Public Education?

A Superintendent of Public Education.

THE GOVERNOR, Lieutenant-Governor, Secretary of State, Attorney-General, State Auditor, and Superintendent of Public Education are elected to serve four years. The State Treasurer is elected two years after the other Executive officers; and his term of office is for four years. The Senate is elected to serve four years, although being so organized that one-half of the Senators vacate every two years. The House of Representatives is elected to serve two years. The Judges of the Supreme Court are appointed by the Governor to serve eight years.

PART I.

HISTORY.

THE EARLY EXPLORERS.

CHAPTER I.

HERNANDO DE SOTO. 1539.

QUESTION. *Who first discovered the Mississippi River?*
ANSWER. Hernando de Soto.

Who was Hernando de Soto?
A Spanish officer, who had been a favorite companion of Pizarro in the conquest of Peru.

From what port did De Soto sail?
From the Bay of Santo Spiritu, in Florida.

When did he leave Santo Spiritu?
May 31, 1539.

Of what did his force consist?
11 vessels ; 1000 infantry, and 350 cavalry.

What was the route taken by De Soto?
Through the present States of Florida, Georgia and Alabama, until after various battles, he attacked Mauvila (near what is now called Mobile), a large fortified Indian town.

Did he capture Mauvila?
Yes, but only after a heroic resistance.

Where did De Soto proceed afterwards?

He wandered, with his army, weakened gradually by disease and battle, during two years, through part of the present States of Alabama, Mississippi, and Tennessee.

Near what point was it that he first saw the Mississippi River?

Near the present city of Memphis.

In what State is Memphis?

When did he first see the river?

Not until two years after leaving Santo Spiritu.

Where did he go afterwards?

He crossed the Mississippi and went up what is now known as White River.

In what State is White River?

What did De Soto do afterwards?

After many hardships, and after having been met by the Indians with alternate hospitality and hostility, he finally reached the mouth of Red River.

In what direction and through what States does Red River flow?

What sorrowful event occurred at that point?

The death of De Soto (May 15, 1542) from a bad fever.

What was done with his body?

It was reverently placed in the trunk of an oak tree, scooped out by his sorrowing companions, and sunk into the waters of the great river which he had been the first to discover.

Near what other point is he supposed to be buried?

Opposite the site of the present town of St. Helena.

In what State is St. Helena?

MARQUETTE DESCENDING THE MISSISSIPPI.

What were De Soto's last words?

"Union and perseverance, my friends! So long as the breath of life animates your bodies, do not falter in the enterprise which you have undertaken."

Did his men carry out his last request?

No, they were afraid to do so.

Why?

They were so annoyed by the warlike Indians who had followed them, that they built boats, and made their way down the Mississippi to the Gulf of Mexico.

How many survivors of De Soto's army returned to Florida?

Only 300; weary, dispirited men—many of whom were badly wounded.

To whom does the honor of the discovery of the Mississippi River, therefore, belong?

To the Spaniards, and to them alone.

CHAPTER II.

FATHER MARQUETTE AND JOLIET. 1673.

How long was it before the next successful attempt to explore the Mississippi River was made?

Not until one hundred and thirty years after De Soto's death.

Who were the leaders?

Father Marquette, a pious monk, and Joliet, an enterprising merchant. They were both Frenchmen.

From what point did they start?

Quebec.

Where is Quebec? When was it founded? By whom?

What course did they take?

They went down the St. Lawrence River—through Lake Ontario—up Niagara River—through Lake Erie—by St. Clair River to Lake Huron—through Lake Huron, by Mackinaw Straits, to and through Fox River to Wisconsin River, down which they proceeded to the Upper Mississippi.

How far down the Mississippi did they go?

Near enough to the mouth to assure themselves that that river flowed into the Gulf of Mexico.

What did they do then?

They returned to Quebec.

What was foreseen by Father Marquette and Joliet?

The vast future importance of the Mississippi River.

———•◦•———

CHAPTER III.

LA SALLE. 1682.

Who was the next discoverer?

Robert Cavalier de la Salle—a French gentleman and soldier.

How long after the Marquette expedition?

Seven years.

From what point did La Salle start?

From Quebec.

What honor may La Salle justly claim?

That of having been the first explorer of the Mississippi River through its whole course, down to the sea.

From what river did he enter the Mississippi River?

From the Illinois River.

When did he first enter the Mississippi?

February 2, 1682.

On what day did he first see the sea?

April 7, 1682.

How many days was he traveling down the Mississippi?

Through how many miles had La Salle passed down among unknown Indian tribes?

Fully 1200 miles.

In whose name did La Salle take possession of the newly discovered country?

In the name of "the most puissant, most high, most invincible and victorious Prince, Louis the Great, King of France."

What name did he give to it?

Louisiana, in honor of the King.

Who was the Louis whom he called the Great?

Louis XIV, King of France.

Did La Salle continue to explore the country?

No, after going up the Mississippi River, he returned shortly to France, where he was received with high honor.

Did La Salle set out again for Louisiana?

Yes, on July 24, 1684, with a fleet of four vessels, given to him by the King, and a considerable army.

What was the object of this second expedition?

He hoped to discover the mouth of the Mississippi River from the sea.

What was the result of this expedition?

It was a complete failure. La Salle never discovered the mouth of the Mississippi from the sea.

On what part of the coast did he land?

On the coast of the Bay of Matagorda, in the present State of Texas.

What was the sad fate of this gallant explorer ?

Abandoned afterwards by most of his companions, he marched for three years through Texas, always seeking the Mississippi River, but never finding it, when he was at last basely murdered, in March, 1687, by his men near Trinity River.

Can you tell whereabout La Salle died ?

About the spot where now stands the town of Washington.

In what State is Washington ?

LA SALLE'S MOST TRUSTED COMPANION AND FRIEND was the Chevalier de Tonti—an Italian officer who had served with distinction in Sicily, where he had lost a hand. For this hand, he substituted one made of copper.

After La Salle's first expedition, the Chevalier remained behind. Nineteen years after, Iberville and Bienville met the gallant De Tonti, who had, during the years which he had passed among the Illinois Indians, greatly endeared himself to them. The Man of the Copper Hand arose to the young Frenchmen of another generation, almost like a ghost from the grave.

CHAPTER IV.

IBERVILLE AND BIENVILLE. 1699.

Who next entered the Mississippi River ?

Iberville and Bienville.

In what year ?

In March, 1699.

Who were Iberville and Bienville?

Two brothers, Canadians by birth, but of French parents—Iberville being the elder and the leader.

Did they discover any land before entering the Mississippi?

Yes ; several islands, among which are those known, to-day, as the Chandeleur Islands, Ship Island and Cat Island.

Can you tell where these islands are situated?

What is said to be the origin of the name " Cat Island"?

When the French first landed, they found there large numbers of a strange animal, which, they said, looked something like a fox and something like a cat. Not knowing what this animal was, one of them exclaimed : "Why ! this must be the kingdom of *cats !*" His companions at once gave the island the name of " Cat Island "—a name which it still retains.

What was this strange animal?

The animal now known as the raccoon.

After entering the Mississippi, where did the brothers go?

As far as the mouth of Red River.

What did they do then?

They descended the river as far as Bayou Manchac, and then separated.

Where did Iberville go?

He passed through Bayou Manchac, and discovered several lakes.

THIS BAYOU is no longer navigable. Later on, in the War of 1812-15, we shall see how it ceased to be so.

What names did he give to these lakes?

One he named Lake Pontchartrain, in honor of Count Pontchartrain, a Minister of France. The other he called Lake Maurepas, after another Minister, Count Maurepas.

What other lake did Iberville discover?

Lake Borgne, which he so called from a French word,

borgne, "one-eyed"—he having found that it was not a complete lake, as it was not entirely surrounded by land.

What other discovery did he make?

He discovered a beautiful bay, which he named Bay St. Louis—after Louis IX, a King of France—who was so good as to be called in history "Saint Louis."

Where did Iberville make his first settlement?

At Biloxi.

Is Biloxi in the present State of Louisiana? If not, where is it?

What gave rise to this name Biloxi?

This was the name of an Indian village which Iberville found on the spot.

Give some account of where Bienville went after leaving Iberville?

He continued down the river to the mouth where the French fleet was moored.

What did he meet before reaching the mouth?

An English vessel, under the command of Capt. Bar.

What reason did Captain Bar give to Bienville for being there?

That he was examining the banks of the river for a proper site for an English colony.

What answer did Bienville make to this?

That Louisiana had already been discovered by the French, and that it was then really a dependency of Canada.

Did the English captain persist in his claim after this?

No; Captain Bar believed Bienville, and, turning back, sailed for the ocean.

What did Bienville name the spot in commemoration of this event?

The "English Turn."

Who can tell where the English Turn is?

After this, what did Bienville do?

He joined Iberville at Biloxi, where he found his brother on the point of leaving for France.

Whom did Iberville appoint Governor of the colony on his return from France?

Another brother, Sauvolle, who was the first Governor of Louisiana—then, on the death of Sauvolle, shortly after, Bienville.

Did Iberville remain long in the colony after this?

No ; after having explored the Mississippi River as far as the site of the present town of Natchez, he returned to France.

What finally became of the gallant Iberville?

After an absence of many years, during which he fought bravely for his king, he had reached the island of San Domingo, on his way to his dear colony which he had never forgotten, when he was attacked with a malignant fever, from which he died in a few hours.

AMONG THE ARRIVALS AT THE NEW COLONY about this time were twenty young girls sent by the French King to be married to the most respectable colonists. The Bishop of Quebec was charged with the duty of selecting in Quebec such young women as were well known to be virtuous. As a proof of her respectability, each one was provided with a curiously worked casket. Hence, as History is fond of giving nicknames wherever it can, these twenty are known in the annals of Louisiana as the CASKET GIRLS.

A few years later, in 1706, the "CASKET GIRLS" became so indignant at being fed on corn bread, that they threatened to leave the colony on the first opportunity ! This was laughingly called the "PETTICOAT INSURRECTION." It ended in nothing.

2

CHAPTER V.

BIENVILLE'S ADMINISTRATION, (FIRST TERM). 1701–1713

Who was left in entire charge of the colony at Biloxi?
Bienville.

Did he remain long in command?
No, the colony was weak ; and many of the colonists, too lazy to work, began to grumble because they did not receive supplies regularly from France. A famine was threatened, and they unjustly blamed Bienville for it.

To what strait were they at last reduced ?
Actually, for a time, to live on acorns.

What was Bienville obliged to do from want of food?
To quarter many of the colonists among the Indians in his neighborhood.

CHAPTER VI.

THE GRANT TO ANTHONY CROZAT. 1713–1718.

What had been done meanwhile in France?
The King, tired of supporting a colony which gave him great trouble, and brought him no revenue, had granted to Anthony Crozat, a wealthy East India merchant, the exclusive right of trading in all the country then known as Louisiana.

For how long was this right given?
For fifteen years from September 14, 1712.

What would this have really made of Crozat?
The master of Louisiana during those fifteen years.

What was the first step taken by him?

He appointed a new Governor in the place of Bienville.

What was the new Governor's name?

Lamotte Cadillac.

What position was given to Bienville?

That of Lieutenant-Governor.

Was Cadillac's administration a success?

No ; he was a great boaster and very quarrelsome. He quarreled with all his subordinate officers—among them, with the noble Bienville.

What petty thing did Cadillac do to show his spite against Bienville?

He sent him on an expedition against the Natchez Indians, who had murdered some Frenchmen near their village (now Natchez).

What was Cadillac's object in doing this?

He hoped that Bienville could not succeed, and that he would either be killed or dishonored by his failure.

How did the expedition end?

It was completely successful.   Bienville caused the ringleaders to be delivered to him, and had them shot.

To the history of what State does this expedition to Natchez belong?

In what did Cadillac's quarrels result?

In his recall in 1716.   He left in disgrace, after having made himself ridiculous both to the whites and the Indians.

Whom did Crozat name as Cadillac's successor?

De L'Epinay.

How did L'Epinay's administration succeed?

No better than Cadillac's.

How did these repeated failures affect Crozat?

Finding that all his plans, either to enrich himself or to improve the colony, had failed, he returned his charter into the King's hands, after he had held it for only five years.

Had the population increased very much during these five years?

Very little. In 1713, it amounted to about 400 persons—20 of whom were blacks. In 1717, there were not more than 700 in all.

To what may this failure be ascribed?

To the general depression among the colonists, and to the fact that most of them preferred rather to starve in the settlements than to live comfortably by planting in the country.

CHAPTER VII.

THE GRANT TO JOHN LAW AND THE MISSISSIPPI COMPANY. FOUNDATION OF NEW ORLEANS. 1718.

To whom did Louis XIV next grant a charter?

To an association generally known as the Mississippi Company.

Who was the Director-General of this Company?

A Scotchman named John Law—a remarkable man —who was also director of the Royal Bank of France.

For how long was this charter conferred?

Twenty-five years.

What was one of its provisions?

The Company, among other things, bound itself, before the charter should expire, to transport to the colony 6,000 whites and 3,000 negroes.

What did John Law boast that he could do for the King?

That he would make him the richest monarch in Europe.

What did he promise to the French people?

That, by means of his Royal Bank, they would have more money than they could spend.

Did he accomplish this boast?

No ; his bank failed after ruining thousands of poor people who had trusted in it.

What became of Law afterwards?

He was driven in disgrace from France, to die later, in absolute want, at Venice.

What was the nickname given to Law's famous Company?

The " MISSISSIPPI BUBBLE ;" because it had grown so big and burst so suddenly.

Who was the first Governor appointed by the Mississippi Company?

Bienville.

Can you tell the year?

In 1718.

What was the first act of Bienville's new administration?

Being dissatisfied with Biloxi, his first act was to select a spot on the Mississippi River as a suitable capital for the colony.

What spot did he choose?

The site of an Indian village, which is that on which New Orleans now stands.

What was the name given by the Indians to their village?

TCHOUTCHOUMA.

What measures did Bienville take to carry out his design?

He left a detachment of 50 men to prepare the ground for building.

Was the seat of government transferred at this time?

This was not done until 1723, five years later.

To what was this delay owing?

To the opposition of the Mississippi Company, which, alarmed by what they had heard of the annual overflow of the Mississippi River, believed that the capital should be on the sea-shore.

To whom, then, must the sole honor of the founding of New Orleans be ascribed?

To the wise and far-seeing Bienville.

Did the Mississippi Company fulfil its contract to send colonists?

In part only. In spite, however, of the death of some and the desertion of many more, the population in 1722 amounted to 5,240 whites and 600 negroes.

Into how many territorial districts was what was then called Louisiana divided?

Nine.

Can you name them?

New Orleans, Biloxi, Mobile, Alabamons (now Alabama), Natchez, Yazoo, Natchitoches, Arkansas and Illinois.

What occurred in the year 1723?

A tremendous hurricane that lasted three days.

Did this hurricane do much damage?

It destroyed the church, the hospital and thirty houses; the shipping in the harbor; and the crops in the country.

What may be observed in connection with hurricanes?

They were more frequent and more violent in those days than they are now.

What was the effect of this disaster upon the colonists?

Most of them were so discouraged that they determined to leave New Orleans. They were, however, finally induced, through Bienville's entreaties, to remain and go to work to rebuild the town.

What was the result of this dissatisfaction?

A conspiracy was formed against Bienville, who was compelled to return to France in January, 1724, to answer the charges made against him.

———————

CHAPTER VIII.

GOVERNOR PERIER'S ADMINISTRATION. 1726 to 1733.

Did Bienville succeed in vindicating himself?

Not at that time ; for he had powerful enemies, who were strong enough, in spite of his innocence, to cause him to lose his office.

Who was the new Governor named by the Mississippi Company?

Périer, in August, 1726.

How was the change received in New Orleans?

With great dissatisfaction—Bienville being greatly loved.

For what was the year 1727 notable?

For the arrival of some Ursuline nuns and some Jesuit priests.

Why did the Ursuline nuns come to New Orleans?

They had been invited to take charge of the Charity Hospital, which had been established there.

What was the object of the Jesuits in coming?

To open schools for the education of the young.

What expedition did Governor Périer undertake in 1727?
He made a tour of the French settlements at Bay St.
Louis, Biloxi, Pascagoula and Mobile.

What did he find the general condition of the colony to be?
Worse than ever. There were few provisions, and
these very dear. The citizens were suffering, and the
soldiers complaining of not being provided by the Company with food or clothing.

What effect did these complaints have upon the Directors?
It caused them to declare that they would no longer
support the heavy expenses of the colony.

How much did the Company say that it had already spent?
20,000,000 livres—about $4,000,000.

To what resolution did it at last come?
To give up the charter as Anthony Crozat had previously done.

In what year was the transfer made?
January, 1731.

Can you state how long the Mississippi Company had controlled the colony?

How long did Périer remain Governor after this?
For about a year. The King reassuming charge of
the colony, recalled him, and once more appointed Bienville as Governor.

What can be said of Périer's character?
That he was an honest man, but of a stern, unyielding disposition, and somewhat rough in manners.

CHAPTER IX.

BIENVILLE'S ADMINISTRATION (SECOND TERM). 1734–1743.

In what war did Bienville find himself engaged at once?

In the war with the Chickasaws.

How many expeditions did he assemble against them?

Two.

What may be said in a few words of these expeditions?

Though led in person by Bienville, they were, owing to various causes—prominent among which was the difficulty of obtaining supplies—unsuccessful.

What occurred on Palm Sunday in the year 1737?

A fearful hail-storm, the hail-stones of which are said to have been as large as common-sized eggs.

How was Bienville impressed by his reverses in war?

He felt himself growing old, and wrote to the Government, asking for his recall.

What reasons did he give for such a request?

He stated that his success in the affairs of his colony had not been such as he had desired, and that, though he had hoped to pass the rest of his days there, a kind of fatality seemed to cling to whatever he did.

How did the King receive Bienville's request?

He acceded to it, and Bienville returned to France.

How does Bienville stand in the history of Louisiana?

As one of its purest and most unselfish rulers. No man ever did so much for the welfare of the colony. No man loved it more.

What title may be given to him?

That of the FATHER OF LOUISIANA.

Can you tell how old Bienville was when he left Louisiana for the last time?

About 65 years old.

How did the colony regard him?

Not only his own people loved him, but the Indian allies honored and revered him.

When, and under what circumstances did he die?

For answer to this, see Chapter XIV.

------◆ ◆ ◆------

CHAPTER X.

DE VAUDREUIL'S ADMINISTRATION. 1743–1753.

Who was named as Bienville's successor?

The Marquis de Vaudreuil.

When did he reach New Orleans?

May 10, 1743.

What order did Governor De Vaudreuil issue to protect the colony against overflow?

That the planters should place their levees in a safe condition under the penalty of forfeiting their lands.

Was this order obeyed?

It was, and this was the beginning of those magnificent levees which are now built along both sides of the great river.

What other decree did the Marquis issue in 1747?

One fixing the precise boundaries of the district of New Orleans.

How did these boundaries run?

They began at the mouth of the Mississippi River, including both banks, up to the German settlement (in the present Parish of St. Charles), above the town, and back of it, as far as Chantilly (now called Gentilly Road).

In what year was the sugar-cane first introduced into the colony?

In 1751.

What number of brick houses were built in New Orleans, the last three years of De Vaudreuil's administration?

Forty-five.

What caused De Vaudreuil's departure at last?

The same dissensions which had been the curse of the colony from its foundation.

Who was his successor?

Gov. Kerlerec.

When did Kerlerec take possession of the Government?

February 9th, 1753.

What became of De Vaudreuil?

He was appointed Governor of Canada, where he distinguished himself for his gallant defence of that Province against the English in 1756.

Can you tell what war that was?

What was his character?

He was a high-toned, and an honorable man. He endeared himself to the colonists by his generosity and liberal hospitality, and was long spoken of among them as the "GREAT MARQUIS."

THE SUGAR CANE was first brought into the colony from Hispaniola, by some Jesuit priests. Seed canes were distributed through the various plantations. Although every effort was made to make the culture profitable, it was not until 1796—45 years afterward—that the cultivation of cane and the manufacture of sugar were successfully introduced.

In Chapter XXIII, the student will find under what circumstances the sugar cane became an Aladdin's Lamp to Louisiana.

CHAPTER XI.

THE NATCHEZ AND CHICKASAW WAR. 1722–1750.

[It has been thought better to place the events connected with the Natchez and Chickasaw war in a separate chapter. Although they were scattered through successive administrations, they form, in fact, one dreary episode of wrongs and bloodshed.]

What was a great drawback to the progress of the Colony?
The frequent wars with the Indians.

What disaster occurred in 1727?
The massacre of the French living at Natchez, by the Natchez Indians.

What caused this massacre?
The unjustifiable cruelty practiced towards the Indians, by the French commander at that post.

What gave greater importance to that event?
In the attempt to avenge the death of their countrymen, the French became involved in a general Indian war.

Name the principal Indian tribes at this time.
The Natchez, the Choctaws and the Chickasaws.

Which of these tribes was the most civilized?
The Natchez.

From what country are the Natchez supposed to have come?
From Mexico.

Did they have any special form of worship?
Yes; they worshiped the sun as their only God.

Where was the Great Village of the Natchez situated?
Near where the present city of Natchez stands.

How many warriors could they bring into the field?
About four thousand.

Which was the most numerous tribe?

The Choctaws.

How many villages did they own; and how many warriors could they muster?

Fifty-two villages ; and ten thousand warriors.

What may be said of the Choctaws?

That they proved generally, the most trusty friends of the French, as the Chickasaws were their fiercest enemies.

Which was regarded as the most warlike tribe?

The Chickasaws.

What was their reputation?

Although not numbering more than 2,500 warriors, they were more feared by the French, and gave more trouble to the colony, than all the other tribes together.

Of what people were the Chickasaws the allies?

The English.

What brought them in conflict with the French?

After the Natchez had been driven from their homes by the French, they took refuge with the Chickasaws, who protected them.

How did these Indian wars affect the colony?

The Indians killed so many of the colonists living in the country, that the survivors, finally, in terror of their lives, fled to New Orleans.

How was this injurious?

The farms were left uncultivated, and the crops perished.

Was the war continuous?

No ; it would stop for a time—sometimes for years— to be renewed with greater fury than ever.

What nation instigated the Indians to continue the contest?

England, the old enemy of the French.

What did the English finally succeed in doing?

In inducing a number of the Choctaws to fight against the French.

Who were more numerous—the Choctaws in favor of the French, or those against them?

The French party was much larger.

How was the Choctaw war ended?

By the skill of a French officer, named Grand Pré, who, at the head of the French Choctaws, gave a crushing defeat to the other party.

Who was finally successful in the general war?

The French, but not until after they had suffered many defeats, sacrificed many lives, and lost much valuable property.

How long did these Indian wars last?

For twenty-eight years, from 1722 to 1750.

Under what Governor did these Indian wars begin?
Under what Governor did they end?

Give an instance of the boldness of the Indians.

Some sportsmen who had gone out to hunt, were killed by them in the immediate neighborhood of New Orleans.

What was the result of the wars?

The Natchez were utterly destroyed, and the power of the Chickasaws was much crippled.

What compliment did Governor De Vaudreuil pay to the Creole soldiers?

He declared them to be the fittest men to fight against the Chickasaws—far better than the French troops.

THE NATCHEZ INDIANS were, by far, the most civilized tribe residing, at the time of the discovery, within the limits of the old Province of Louisiana.

Their real origin dated back beyond the memory even of tradition. Their wise men spoke fancifully of their ancestors having come from a land close to that glowing Sun which they worshiped. Where that country was, none of them knew. They told the French that, between the Land of the Sun and their home on the great River, where they made their last desperate stand, their fathers, in the old time, had stopped in Mexico. Who can tell when and during how many years the Natchez stayed in Mexico? "That happened many, many Suns before our time,"—that was all their old men said.

The Natchez were far ahead of the other Indian tribes in their system of government. Their king exercised supreme authority. He was called the "GREAT SUN." He was reverenced next to the Great Sun, his Brother, shining in heaven. The members of the Royal Family—numbering 500 persons—were called "Suns." The Natchez had their gentry, or men of consideration, who made the second class. Their third and last class were known as *miche quipy*, common people.

The Natchez were gentle in their bearing, and very grave and wise in council. They were brave warriors, but they were men of peace, instead of war. It was their wars that had driven them ages back, from the Land of the Sun into Mexico. It was their wars that had forced them to leave Mexico to form a new civilization upon the banks of a river, which was inhabited only by savage and hostile tribes.

The Natchez were remarkable for their stature. The men were tall and symmetrical. Very few of them were less than six feet high. The smallest man known to the French measured five feet. He was looked upon as a dwarf, and was ashamed to show his face among the men of his tribe.

CHAPTER XII.

KERLEREC'S ADMINISTRATION. 1753–1763.

What had Kerlerec been before being appointed governor?
A captain in the French Navy.

What was the opinion he formed of the army of the colony?
He found the Swiss soldiers superior to the French.

What did he do in consequence of his opinion?
He wrote to the Government suggesting that the French companies should be reduced in number and their places supplied by the Swiss.

What was the proportion of these troops in New Orleans?
900 French and 75 Swiss.

What made Kerlerec anxious at this time?
The unprotected state of the colony, and the threatened attack by the English.

What justified this anxiety?
The fact that the English had recently attacked the French in Canada, and were threatening the entire French settlements in America.

Can you tell anything about this war in Canada in 1756 ?

Did Kerlerec take any measures against the danger?
He did all he could. He established a force of scouts at Cat Island ; strengthened the fortifications at the English Turn ; and urged the Government to send a reinforcement of 500 soldiers.

What precautions meanwhile did he take in New Orleans?
He had it surrounded by a ditch-palisade.

Were his appeals to the Government attended to?
No ; Louis XV, who had succeeded Louis XIV, was

not a warlike King like his grandfather. During his reign, neither France nor her colonies prospered.

What were the English doing all this time?

They kept a number of armed privateers around the mouth of the Mississippi River.

What injury did they do to the French by this?

By means of the blockade, the English cut off all communication between France and the colony for three years.

When did the first vessel reach New Orleans?

In August, 1758. It brought a new commissary, who was provided with supplies and clothing for the colony.

What soon resulted from his arrival?

The old story. Governor Kerlerec and the new commissary were soon on bad terms. Kerlerec complained to the king that the commissary was dishonest, and the commissary declared that the governor was corrupt.

What did the king do?

He recalled the commissary first, and afterwards Kerlerec himself.

Who was appointed Kerlerec's successor?

Abbadie, who reached New Orleans, June 29, 1763.

How long had Kerlerec been governor?

About ten years and five months.

What became of him on his return to France?

He was accused of having violated his duty, and was thrown into the Bastile.

THE BASTILE was a famous prison for political prisoners in Paris. It was destroyed by the mob during the French Revolution. Its last stone was knocked down; and it was regretted by no one.

CHAPTER XIII.

THE CESSION TO SPAIN. 1763.

What important event occurred during Kerlerec's administration?

The cession, by France to Spain, of the colony of Louisiana.

What was the cause of the cession?

Louis XV, like his grandfather Louis XIV, like Crozat and the Mississippi Company, had grown tired of paying the expenses of a colony which brought him nothing.

How did Spain receive the offer made by France?

At first, very unwillingly. She declared that she had too many colonies already. Finally, however, on King Louis urging her to do so, that country consented to accept the gift.

When was the Treaty of Cession signed by Spain?

February 10th, 1763.

What other country was made a party to the treaty?

England.

What did Spain receive on the West side of the Mississippi River?

All the vast territory extending from its mouth to its utmost tributaries.

What did she receive on the East bank?

The city of New Orleans, and the surrounding country, extending from the mouth of the Mississippi to the Iberville River (now Bayou Manchac), thence, by an imaginary line, drawn in the middle of that stream, through Lakes Maurepas and Pontchartrain, back to the Gulf of Mexico.

What was England's share?

The port and river of Mobile, and all the country on the East bank of the Mississippi from its source to the Iberville River. It was by this same treaty that Canada was ceded to England.

NOTE. The teacher should make himself certain here that the class understands perfectly, *on the map*, what was Spain's share and what was England's.

Can you point out on the map England's share ?

How were the colonists pleased with this cession ?

Not at all ; they protested strongly against it.

How did the Indian allies receive it ?

They were very angry. They declared that the King of France had no right to transfer them to any new white chief, like so much cattle.

What did many of the tribes do ?

They came to New Orleans with all their goods, and were granted lands on the West bank of the Mississippi.

During all this time what was Spain doing ?

Nothing.

What do you infer from this ?

That Spain was not very anxious to take possession of her new colony.

How did the colony first receive an official notice of the transfer?

By a letter from Louis XV himself to Governor Abbadie.

When was this letter announced in New Orleans?

In October, 1764.

How Florida was Divided. At this time, what was known as Florida, which was a Spanish colony, was' divided into two governments. These divisions were called " East Florida " and " West Florida."

East Florida was retained by Spain, with St. Augustine as its capital.

West Florida with the Mississippi River, north of the Iberville, as its western boundary. and the mouth of the Yazoo River as its northern limit, was included within the territory ceded to England. Pensacola was made its capital.

Let the pupil remember this when the Spanish Governor Galvez shall, a few years later, lead his soldiers and ships against Pensacola.

CHAPTER XIV.

THE CESSION TO SPAIN.   ULLOA'S ARRIVAL AND EXPULSION.   1765–1768.

What event occurred in 1765?

The death of Governor Abbadie, who was much liked in the colony.

Was his successor a Frenchman or a Spaniard?

A Frenchman, Captain Aubry, an officer who had previously distinguished himself at Fort Duquesne.

What do you know of the attack on Fort Duquesne?

What did the inhabitants of the colony do after receiving the official announcement of the cession?

They met in convention at New Orleans, and agreed

upon a resolution, appealing to Louis not to separate them from the mother-country.

Whom did they make the bearer of their petition?

Jean Milhet—the richest merchant in the colony.

Whom did Milhet first consult on his arrival in Paris?

Bienville, who was at the time in his 86th year, and very weak in body, although strong in mind.

What did Bienville do to assist him?

He accompanied Milhet to see the Prime Minister, De Choiseul, and begged him, with tears in his eyes, to allow Louisiana to remain under the French Government.

What was the Minister's answer?

He replied that he could do nothing, because, if Louisiana continued to belong to France, it would be certainly seized by the English, with whom the French were always at war.

How did the rejection affect Bienville?

So deeply that after leaving the minister's cabinet, the good old man fell sick and died, in a few days, from grief.

How long did the Spanish Government delay sending a governor to New Orleans?

For nearly a year, when it appointed Don Antonio de Ulloa governor.

Did Ulloa come at once to New Orleans?

No ; he remained at Havana for nearly a year.

When did he at last reach New Orleans?

March 5, 1766.

How long was this after the signing of the Treaty of Cession?

How was he received by the Louisianians?

Very coldly.

What did Ulloa decline to do?

He declined to show, as he was asked to do, his commission as governor to the Superior Council of New Orleans.

What was the ground of his refusal?

That he had nothing at all to do with that body, but only with Captain Aubry, the French governor.

What other reason did Ulloa give for this course?

That he would not take formal possession of the country, until the Spanish troops which he expected should arrive.

What was the population of the colony at this time?

By a census ordered by Ulloa, it was estimated at 10,004 persons in all—half of whom were colored. There were 1,893 men able to carry arms.

How did Governor Ulloa seem disposed towards the colonists?

Very kindly at first. His reports to his Government were all friendly.

In what way did the colonists look upon him?

With great bitterness. They opposed almost every measure suggested by him.

What especially excited their indignation?

A certain law regulating commerce, which Ulloa had been ordered by his government to enforce.

Did he proclaim the law himself?

No; but through Aubry, who was still acting as French governor.

How did the colonists show their disapproval of the law?

A petition complaining of Governor Ulloa's administration was signed by over 1,000 citizens. They rose in arms and paraded the streets.

What body did the citizens find ready to assist them?

The Superior Council, which had been displeased by the Spanish governor's course towards it.

What did the Council do?

It met, and on October 29, 1768, decreed that Ulloa should leave the colony within three days.

How did Governor Aubry act in this emergency?

Like an honest man. Fearing that some violence might be done to Gov. Ulloa, he accompanied him and his family, with a few French troops who had remained true to him, to a Spanish man-of-war, the *Volante,* then lying in front of the city.

Did Ulloa leave within the time specified by the Council?

Yes; sailing on November 1, 1768, for Havana.

How long had Governor Ulloa been in Louisiana?

How many ringleaders were there in the revolution?

Twelve—the chief of whom was one Lafrenière, the French king's Attorney-General. Among them was the same Jean Milhet, whom the colonists had sent to Paris as their ambassador.

GOVERNOR ULLOA'S COMMERCIAL REGULATION was one confining the trade of the colony to six Spanish ports, viz.: Seville, Alicant, Carthagena, Malaga, Barcelona and Coruna.

Vessels were prohibited from engaging in the trade, unless they were either Spanish-built, or commanded by Spaniards.

This was a bad regulation, because it not only broke up an active trade already established with French ports, but imposed heavy expenses of transportation, which, as the colonists complained, swallowed up all their profits.

THE CHIEFS OF THE REVOLUTION were among the most influential citizens of New Orleans.

They loved France better than France loved Louisiana. They believed that a mother-country was as much bound to take care of her colonies, as a good mother is to protect her children.

This was a sad mistake. The end for them made the mistake sadder.

CHAPTER XV.

GENERAL O'REILLY'S ARRIVAL. THE TRIAL OF LAFRENIERE AND HIS COMPANIONS. 1769.

What course did Governor Aubry pursue after Ulloa's departure?

He wrote to the French Government, without delay, informing it of all that had happened.

What measures of defence did the citizens take?

They sent also their own statement, defending their action, and begging Louis to receive them back under his authority.

What reply did Louis give?

A cold refusal.

Who was the King of Spain at this time?

Charles III, an able king, and a just man.

What was the course taken by Charles?

He at once called a Council of his Ministers at Madrid.

To what decision did the Ministers come?

That Spain should retain possession of Louisiana, in spite of what had occurred.

What was the final conclusion of the Spanish King?

To send to New Orleans an army large enough to chastise the insult to the Spanish crown, and to enforce its authority in the colony.

Who was appointed Governor and General of the army?

General Alexander O'Reilly.

What was General O'Reilly's reputation?

That of a brave and gallant officer, of the highest

rank in the Spanish army, and in King Charles' confidence.

*How did the citizens of New Orleans receive the news of
the formidable preparations of Spain?*

Already disheartened by the French king's rejection
of their petition, they were thrown into a state of great
alarm.

When did General O'Reilly reach New Orleans?

He made his appearance with his fleet, and entered
the city on August 18th, 1769.

Of how many vessels did his fleet consist?

Of twenty-four sail, containing an army of 2,600 men,
among the best troops in the Spanish army.

What step did O'Reilly first take?

To order the arrest of Lafrenière and the other
chiefs of the revolution.

How did the people receive the news of these arrests?

They were seized with terror. They deserted the
streets and closed the doors of their houses.

How did O'Reilly quiet their fears?

By a proclamation, declaring that only those who had
led the colonists in the insurrection would be punished.

Did the trial proceed?

Yes ; all the prisoners, with the exception of one who
died in prison on the day of his arrest, were brought to
trial.

THIS WAS VILLERE, the ancestor of one of the most honorable
families in Louisiana, who died. His death is said to have been
caused by apoplexy.

What was the verdict of the court?

All were found guilty.

3

Were all condemned to the same punishment?

No ; six of them, Lafrenière among them, were sentenced to be hanged as the chief leaders. The others were sentenced to various terms of imprisonment, from six to ten years, and forbidden ever to live within the Spanish dominions.

Was the sentence of hanging carried out?

It was not. No hangman could be found, and those condemned to death were ordered to be shot.

THE PUBLIC HANGMAN. An interesting story is connected with the appointment of the first hangman for the colony.

In the days of the Mississippi Company, JEANNOT, one of its slaves, was offered his freedom on condition of acting as hangman. Jeannot appeared to accept the offer. However, there was nothing farther from his heart. He requested permission to go to a distance. Once there, he deliberately seized a hatchet and cut off his right arm. Then he returned and showed his bleeding stump. *He* could not serve as hangman.

Jeannot received his reward. He was appointed overseer of all the slaves belonging to the company. He lived and died honored by the entire colony.

In the case of Lafrenière and his companions, no man, white or black, was base enough to act the part of hangman of the gallant patriots.

What may be said of this verdict?

Though Lafrenière and his companions had openly conspired against the Spanish Government, the sentence approved by General O'Reilly was, under the circumstances, a most cruel one.

What more may be said of it?

It has remained ever since a dark stain upon the memory of General O'Reilly.

What became of the companions of those shot?

They were taken to Havana and imprisoned in the

Morro Castle, but they were soon released by the Spanish king.

THIS RELEASE was due to the son of Masan—one of the condemned. Young Masan threw himself at the feet of King Charles, and nobly pleaded to be allowed to take his unhappy father's place. The king was so touched by this evidence of filial love that he, at once, ordered the discharge of all the prisoners.

What was the fate of Governor Aubry?

Shortly after O'Reilly's arrival, he left Louisiana for Bordeaux in France. The vessel had already reached the river Garonne, when it was wrecked, and Aubry, among others, was lost.

What touching evidence of fidelity is told of two slaves?

Artus, a cook and a confiscated slave of Lafrenière, and Cupidon, a house-servant, who had belonged to Caresse, another of the executed leaders, on General O'Reilly's ordering them to perform their special duties in his own household, refused on the ground that *" they would never serve their master's assassin."*

CHAPTER XVI.

O'REILLY'S ADMINISTRATION. 1769–1770.

What did O'Reilly do, after the execution of Lafrenière, to restore the confidence of the people?

He sent away the larger number of the Spanish troops.

How many did he retain?

About 1,200 soldiers.

How many had been sent away?

To what effect was the next proclamation issued by him?

By proclamation, November 25, 1769, O'Reilly abolished the tribunal known as the Superior Council.

What reason did he assign for this step?

The conduct of the Council during the revolution against Governor Ulloa.

What body did Governor O'Reilly establish in its place?

One known as the *Cabildo.*

What was the Cabildo?

A body consisting of nine officials, and a clerk—presided over by the Governor himself.

Was the colony permitted to remain under the French laws?

No ; O'Reilly was ordered by the Spanish king to govern it by the same laws which prevailed in the other Spanish provinces.

What was the colony farther made?

A dependency of the Island of Cuba.

What can be said of O'Reilly's policy towards the French colonists?

It was, after the execution of the revolutionists, generally, both friendly and impartial.

Why does it deserve to be so called?

O'Reilly, in selecting the members of the *Cabildo,* appointed Frenchmen to many of the positions.

How else did he show his desire to conciliate the colonists?

By retaining, almost without exception, the French commandants at the various posts.

What excellent commercial regulations were recommended by General O'Reilly to the king?

The establishment of free trade with Cuba.

What articles were included in this traffic?

To use O'Reilly's own words : "The colony wants flour, wine, oil, instruments, arms, ammunition and every sort of manufactured goods for clothing and other domestic purposes."

What were the productions which the colony had to exchange for these goods?

Timber, indigo, cotton, furs, and a small quantity of corn and rice.

What may be said of O'Reilly's policy to the Spanish Indians?

It was marked by justice. He used his best exertions to prevent them from being cheated by the whites, and to urge them to live in friendship with other tribes.

Had General O'Reilly come to the colony with the intention of remaining?

No; he had been temporarily appointed, merely to punish the insult to the Spanish crown, and to restore public order. He was directed, after having accomplished those purposes, to return to Spain.

When did he leave New Orleans?

October 29, 1770.

How long had O'Reilly been in Louisiana?

What is the character with which General O'Reilly has come down to posterity?

That of a gallant officer, an honorable man, and with the single exception of his severity toward the French revolutionists, a mild and just Governor.

CHAPTER XVII.

UNZAGA'S ADMINISTRATION. 1770–1777.

Whom did O'Reilly leave as Governor of Louisiana?

Don Louis de Unzaga.

In what capacity had Unzaga first come to the colony?

As Colonel of the Regiment of Havana. He was confirmed as Governor only later, in August, 1772.

Who arrived in the beginning of 1772?

A priest and two assistants who were sent, at the king's expense, to teach the young Louisianians the Spanish language.

Had O'Reilly's recommendations for Free Trade been attended to by the king?

Yes, in August, 1772 ; but so partially that it did not prove very advantageous to the colony.

What course did Governor Unzaga take on his own responsibility?

He allowed the colony to trade openly with the English on the Mississippi River.

What had the English been doing previously?

Carrying on an active smuggling trade.

What had been one of their devices?

They had turned two large vessels into floating stores. It was their habit to stop these vessels along the bank, making fast to a tree, and tempt every man with a sight of their goods.

In what way was Unzaga's action useful?

It enabled the people, who could not otherwise get supplies, to buy them from the English without fear of punishment.

What is to be remarked of the winter of 1772?

That it was the severest known to the colonists, after the winters of 1748 and 1766.

Give an instance of the force of the terrible hurricane in that year.

A British schooner was driven to Cat Island, where the waters rose so high that they carried her bodily over the island.

With what nation did Unzaga fear trouble in 1776?

With England.

To what was this owing?

To the war then going on between England and her American colonies.

What had made Governor Unzaga anxious?

A number of American merchants from Boston, New York and Philadelphia, who were then in New Orleans, had succeeded in sending from that town a large supply of arms and ammunition to the patriots of Western Pennsylvania.

Had this been done with the Spanish Governor's knowledge?

It had, and Governor Unzaga feared that the English would call him to account for it.

Who was most active among the Americans?

Oliver Pollock, an enterprising merchant.

Did England take any action in the matter?

None at all. She found the Americans to be all that she could manage for eight long years.

What honor was conferred upon the Governor during this year?

He was made Brigadier-General in the Spanish army.

How did he receive this promotion?

Not very cheerfully, for he petitioned the king to be allowed to retire from the colony with the pay of Colonel.

What reasons did he give for his request?

His advanced age, and the bad state of his health.

With what success did his petition meet?

King Charles granted it so far as to permit him to leave Louisiana; but he declined to allow him to leave active service.

Was this decision complimentary, or not, to Unzaga?

What honorable appointment did the king confer on him on leaving New Orleans?

That of Captain-General of Caraccas.

Where is Caraccas? (See the map of South America.)

What may be said of Unzaga's administration as Governor?

It was throughout more that of a wise and indulgent father than a ruler, and gained for him the affection of the entire colony.

How long was Unzaga Governor?

CHAPTER XVIII.

GALVEZ'S ADMINISTRATION. 1777–1783.

Whom did Unzaga leave as Governor on his departure, February 1, 1777?

Don Bernardo de Galvez.

What was Galvez at the time?

Colonel of the Regiment of Louisiana.

What is there peculiar about his appointment?

He was the youngest governor Louisiana ever had.

Why do you say so?

He was not more than twenty-one years old, when he entered upon his high duties.

What can you say with regard to Galvez's parentage?

He belonged to one of the most powerful families in Spain.   His father was Viceroy of Mexico, and an uncle was King Charles' chief and favorite minister.

What prudent move was taken by the Governor concerning the commerce of the colony?

He allowed the colonists to export their produce to

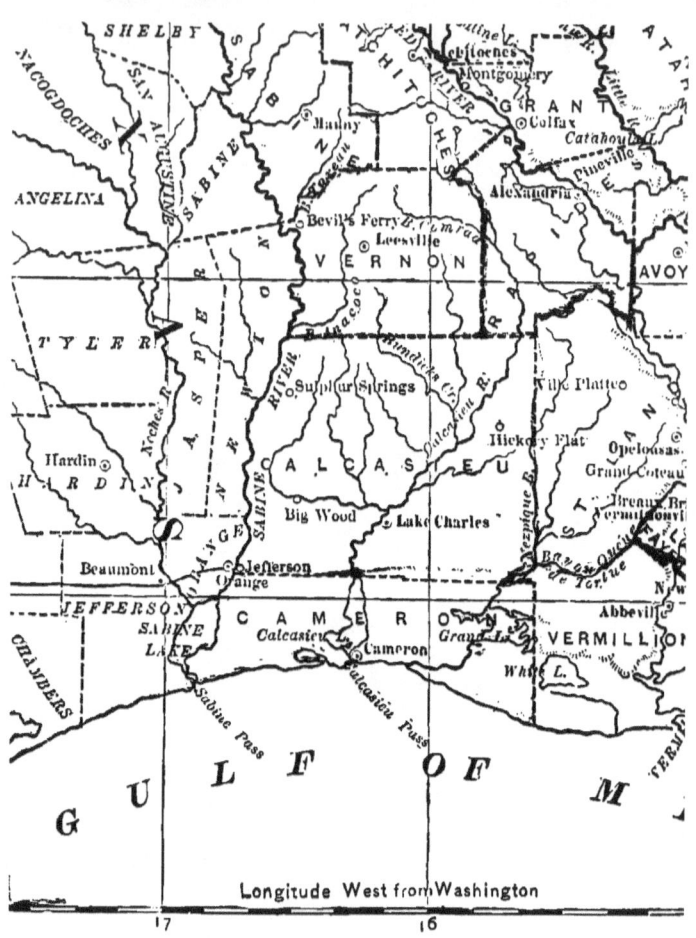

Longitude West from Washington

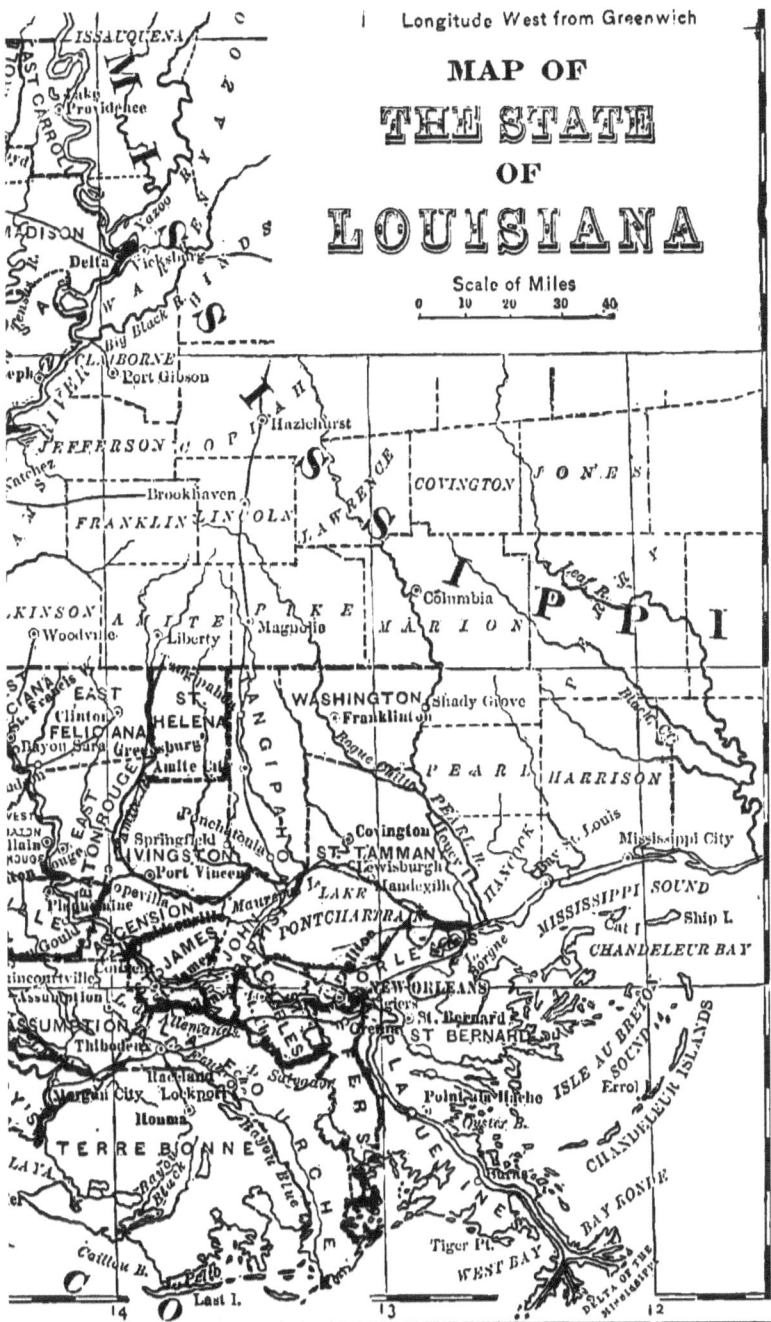

Longitude West from Greenwich

MAP OF

THE STATE

OF

LOUISIANA

Scale of Miles

0   10   20   30   40

N. Y. Map and Relief-Line Eng. Co., 17 Warren St.

any of the French ports—a privilege that had been refused to them since the days of Governor Ulloa.

How did this extension of the trade affect the colony?

Very beneficially, in reviving the hopes of the people, and enabling them to get better prices for their products.

What other fortunate event occurred in 1778?

The arrival of a number of families, sent, at the Spanish king's expense, from the Canary Islands.

THE CANARY ISLAND COLONISTS remained only a few days in New Orleans. They soon scattered themselves over the colony. Some, under the command of Marigny de Mandeville,—one of the most famous of the early Louisianians—settled in the present Parish of St. Bernard. Others made a settlement twenty-four miles from what is now the city of Baton Rouge. The remainder established themselves on Bayou Lafourche.

In January, 1799, some five hundred more arrived from the Canaries. These were taken to the Attakapas District, and made their homes on the banks of the beautiful Bayou Teche.

Where are the Canary Islands? [See Map of Europe.]

How are the descendants of these colonists known to-day?

Under the name of *Islingues*—a name derived from the Spanish word *Isleños* (meaning islanders).

What has contributed to make Governor Galvez's Administration one of the most famous in the history of Louisiana?

His brilliant military enterprises against the English posts during the American Revolution.

In what way was Louisiana brought into that war?

France, the ally of Spain, having recognized the independence of the United States, Spain, after having her propositions for peace rejected by England, declared war against that country, May 8, 1779.

How was the news of hostilities received by Gov. Galvez?

He hailed it with joy.

3*

Why?

He was young and thirsted for military glory.

What did he do?

He at once planned an attack upon the English posts at Bayou Manchac, Baton Rouge, and Natchez, which he submitted to a council of war for their approval.

What did the council advise?

They were timid, rejected the proposition, and recommended him to suspend all plans of attack until the arrival of reinforcements from Havana.

Was Galvez inclined to follow this advice?

No ; he at once resolved to act on his own responsibility.

How did he proceed?

He called a mass-meeting of the inhabitants of New Orleans, and, after telling them that war had been declared by Spain against England, and that they must defend themselves against the English, exclaimed : " Will you stand by me, and conquer or die with your governor and for your king ? "

What answer did the people give to this?

They tendered their lives for the defence of Louisiana and for the service of the king.

FIFTEEN HUNDRED YOUNG CREOLES responded to Galvez's appeal of " *Let those who love me follow where I lead.*" Through all the fortunes of the war, they remained faithful to their brilliant young Governor.

CHAPTER XIX.

GALVEZ'S ADMINISTRATON (CONTINUED). THE WAR AGAINST THE ENGLISH. 1779.

What was Galvez's first step?

He put all the provisions, ammunition and artillery into one small schooner and three gun-boats, which he directed to ascend the river, while his army marched along the banks.

When did the army leave New Orleans?

August 27, 1779.

Who commanded it?

It was commanded by the Governor himself, with Don Estevan Miro, as next in rank.

What was its strength on starting out?

It consisted of 170 regular soldiers and 330 recruits; 30 carbiniers; 60 militiamen; a company of 80 free colored men; 9 American volunteers, led by Oliver Pollock, the agent of the American Congress.

What reinforcements did Galvez receive on the way?

Six hundred volunteers, white and colored, besides 160 Indians who had been gathered up at the different settlements, the whole forming a body of 1,430 men.

What was the first English post attacked?

Fort Manchac, situated about 130 miles from New Orleans. Its garrison being small, it was carried by storm on September 7th.

What place did Galvez next capture?

The fort of Baton Rouge. It was strongly fortified and defended by 400 regulars and 100 militiamen. The fort and garrison surrendered, September 21, after a bombardment of ten hours.

What was one of the conditions imposed by Galvez on the garrison at Baton Rouge?

That Fort Panmure, at Natchez, should be delivered up to the Spaniards.

Was this condition complied with?

It was ; and the fort surrendered with its entire garrison of eighty grenadiers.

During these movements on land, what was being done on the water?

Several English vessels were captured by greatly inferior forces.

What were the most important of these captures?

That of the English privateer " West Florida," by an American named Pikle, on Lake Pontchartrain ; and the boarding and capture, by Vincent Rieux, a native of New Orleans, assisted by thirteen other Creoles, of an English bark, well armed, and carrying fifty-four grenadiers and their officers, and ten or twelve sailors.

THIS WAS a most gallant exploit. Rieux and his men were hailed everywhere as heroes.

Name the general results of this gallant campaign.

The capture of eight vessels and three forts ; five hundred and fifty-six regulars, including Lieut. Col. Dickenson, the British commander-in-chief, and many sailors and militiamen. The Spanish loss was very slight.

How did the Creole militia behave?

With great discipline and fortitude.

What volunteers were particularly bitter against the English?

The Acadians.

For reason for this, see Chapter V. of the Geography, page

What did Galvez say about the colored companies?

That they had acted with as much valor as the whites.

What was observed of the Indian allies?

That they had refrained from all violence toward the prisoners.

What instance can you give of this?

Many of them brought in their arms, to the Governor, little children who had taken refuge in the woods with their mothers.

What did Galvez do after the capture of Fort Panmure?

He returned to New Orleans where he allowed the militia to go to their homes.

———◆◆◄———

CHAPTER XX.

GALVEZ'S ADMINISTRATION (CONTINUED). 1780.

What occurred in October?

The arrival of a reinforcement of Spanish troops from Havana.

What did this arrival induce Galvez to plan?

An expedition against Mobile. He was enthusiastically assisted in his preparations by the Creoles, who had now the greatest confidence in their young Governor.

When did the expedition start?

It sailed from the Balize, Feb. 5, 1780.

What was its strength?

Two thousand men, regulars, militia and some companies of colored men.

Did the English at Mobile offer any resistance?
Very little, the garrison not being large.

Why was Galvez fortunate in securing so prompt a surrender?
Because Gen. Campbell, the English commander at Pensacola, a few days after, arrived near Mobile with a force sufficient to have saved the fort. But it not being strong enough to retake the fort from the Spaniards, he returned with his army to Pensacola without doing anything.

Against what point did Galvez next propose to move?
Against Pensacola, the strongest of the English posts.

Where did he go to organize an army for this expedition?
To Havana.

What became of the first expedition?
It was dispersed in a violent hurricane, a number of vessels foundered, and Galvez was compelled to return to Havana with the remnant.

Was Galvez discouraged by this misfortune? '
No; he at once organized another and a stronger force and left Havana, February 28, for Pensacola.

Of what was the second army composed?
One ship of the line and two frigates, under the command of a Spanish admiral, and several transports on which were 1,400 soldiers, with ample artillery.

What was his first step on reaching the neighborhood of Pensacola?
He found that where the vessels were outside the bar, they were in danger from storms. He, therefore, called upon the admiral of the Spanish fleet to consult his captains as to the best way of getting the ships over the bar into a safe place.

What was the reply of those officers?

That they thought that any attempt to cross the bar would expose the fleet to a raking fire from the English forts inside, and that any attack, by water, on the British would be fruitless.

Of what similar event in Galvez's own career does this action of the Admiral remind you?

What was Galvez's course after this timid counsel?

He waited for a few days, when Don Estevan Miró arrived in charge of the Creole troops. He then took a brig, a schooner and two small gunboats—all the naval force of which Louisiana could boast—and, in spite of a heavy fire poured upon his little fleet, he succeeded in landing safely at the lower part of the bay.

What effect did this heroic achievement have upon the Spanish Admiral and his officers?

Fired by Galvez's example, and afraid of being dishonored if they remained behind, they crossed the bar with the fleet and joined his forces.

When did the attack on Pensacola begin?

In the beginning of April, a simultaneous fire was opened by both the fleet and the army upon the forts, and was continued day after day.

Did this bombardment make any impression?

Very little, as the English fortifications were unusually strong.

What finally compelled the English to surrender?

The merest accident.

What was this accident?

In the first week of May, a powder magazine blew up in the fort. A breach was thus made, through which Galvez sent a strong detachment which took possession of the redoubt, and opened a fire upon the English with their own guns.   Galvez himself, at the head of the army, was preparing to storm, when the garrison surrendered.

How many men did General Campbell surrender ?
More than 800 regulars.

What was the result of this victory?
The whole province of West Florida remained in the hands of the Spaniards.

WEST FLORIDA, as the pupil will see, has once more fallen into the possession of the Spaniards, It was ceded to England in 1764 [See Note Chapter XIII].

Thus, when Governor Galvez captured Pensacola, the capital of British Florida, he merely restored West Florida to the country to which most of it had originally belonged.

The Spain of those days never forgot the services of her gallant sons. And Galvez—one of the most gallant of her sons—was soon rewarded with higher honors. No Spanish Governor in Louisiana could ever lay such claims to such honors.

What reasons have the Louisianians to be proud of their action in this campaign ?
That they too, though under the Spanish flag, *assisted the Americans in their struggle for independence.*

What reward did Galvez receive for the capture of Pensacola ?
He was promoted to the grade of Lieutenant-General, and appointed Captain-General of the provinces of Louisiana and Florida.

When was the Treaty of Peace signed between Great Britain, the United States and Spain ?
September 3, 1783.

What did Spain gain by this treaty ?
West Florida was secured to her.

What privileg in connection with the Mississippi River did the United States gain by it ?
The navigation of the Mississippi, from its source to its mouth, was declared free and open to their citizens.

What is to be remarked of the winter of 1783-84?
That it was a very severe one.

Give an instance of its extreme severity.
The whole river in front of New Orleans was filled with fragments of floating ice, mostly from twelve to thirty feet long, and two to three feet thick. All communication between the two banks was interrupted between the 13th and 19th of February, 1784.

THIS IS THE ONLY TIME, probably, that ice of such proportions has been seen floating down the Mississippi as far as New Orleans.

When did Galvez leave the colony, and how?
His father dying in the summer of 1785, he succeeded him as Viceroy of Mexico, and at once proceeded to his new post.

When did he die?
In 1794, aged 38 years.

What had been the character of Galvez's administration?
Mild, just, and enlightened.

What was his character as a soldier?

———•◆•———

CHAPTER XXI.

MIRO'S ADMINISTRATION. 1785-1792.

Who succeeded Galvez as Governor?
Don Estevan Miró.

Who was Miro?

What became the new title of the Spanish Governors from this time?
Governor of the Provinces of Louisiana and West Florida.

No Better Proof can be given of the satisfaction that Spain really felt, in once more securing possession of the Province of West Florida, than this addition to the title and authority of the Governors of Louisiana. By it, she declared emphatically her purpose to maintain her hold over the Province.

Let not the pupil forget this, when Louisiana is ceded back by Spain to France in 1803; when France sells "Louisiana" to the United States; and when the United States are not quite sure whether they have bought West Florida, or not, but on the whole, think that they have, and are going to stand by what they think.

What was the population of New Orleans in 1785?

Four thousand eight hundred and ninety, and that of the whole colony, including Mobile and Natchez, 31,433.

As the population in 1769 was 13,538; how much had it gained?

What cause of trouble did Governor Miró have at first?

The Americans complained that they were not allowed the free navigation of the Mississippi River, as had been promised by the Treaty; but that, when they brought their produce down the river, they were compelled to pay larger sums, as duties to the Spaniards, than they could afford.

What did they call the Mississippi?

The highway to the sea given to them by God, which they were resolved to have and to keep free.

What did they threaten to do?

They threatened to invade Louisiana and seize New Orleans.

How did Miró meet these threats?

He wrote to the Spanish Government, urging upon it to strengthen the defences of Louisiana. At the same time, he reduced the duties of Western produce as much as he could.

How was the reduction received by the Western people?
It satisfied them for a time, but for a time only.

CHAPTER XXII.

MIRO'S ADMINISTRATION (CONTINUED). 1787–1792.

What dangerous scheme was formed in 1787 ?
One to break up the new American Union, by inducing the people of the territory of Kentucky to secede
from it, and to put themselves under the protection of
Spain.

Who was the leader of this movement on the American side?
General James Wilkinson, who had been a brave
officer in the Revolution.

Who conducted it on the Spanish side?
Governor Miró himself.

What was the basis of this scheme?
Kentucky, which had been a portion of the territory
of the State of Virginia, had petitioned Congress to
allow it to become an independent State. That body
had delayed doing so.

Why did Congress not grant the petition at once?
Because, at this time, the United States were preparing a new Constitution ; and it was justly thought that
the Constitution should be in operation before new
States were admitted under it.

What effect did this delay have upon some Kentuckians?
A party declared that Congress meant to deceive them,
and clamored for separation from the United States.

Was that all that General Wilkinson wanted?
No ; for he had promised Miró that Kentucky would

first become an independent Republic, and that, afterwards, he would so manage that she should place herself under Spanish protection.

What would have been the result of this?

That the Kentuckians would have ceased to be American citizens, and would have become Spanish subjects.

In what manner did he go to work to carry out this wicked design?

Very cautiously. He knew that a large majority of the people of Kentucky were faithful to the Union. So he intrigued secretly among the more prominent men, and got some of them to promise him their support.

Was Wilkinson doing this as a patriot?

Far from it. He was acting for his own selfish advantage.

GENERAL WILKINSON is said, during this whole time, to have been receiving a regular salary from the King of Spain. No patriotic American should accept the money of another Government, as a reward for attempting to destroy his own.

How did Miró help the scheme?

By offering liberal advantages—land free, no taxes to pay, etc., to all who would emigrate and settle in Louisiana.

Did any Americans avail themselves of these privileges?

Yes, several hundred families—a number of whom settled in the Feliciana district.

What caused the Kentucky plot to be at last abandoned?

The admission of Kentucky into the Union as a State.

How did this cause its supporters to cease their intrigues?

Because Kentucky—once admitted as a State of the American Union—had gained all the rights and privileges which she had asked for.

How long had this conspiracy been carried on?
Four years, from 1787 to 1791.

What emigrants arrived in 1791?
Refugees from the French island of St. Domingo (West Indies) who had been driven away by a revolution.

Who came among these refugees?
A company of actors, who opened the first regular theatre that had ever been seen in New Orleans.

When did Governor Mirò leave Louisiana?
At the close of 1791.

In what condition was the colony?
Entirely reconciled to the Spanish rule.

To what was this largely owing?
To the wise and kindly policy of most of the Spanish governors.

Can you tell me something peculiar connected with them?
Several of them—such as Governors Unzaga, Galvez, and Mirò, had married Creole ladies. It appears strange to say that none of the French governors had ever done so ; but such was the case.

CHAPTER XXIII.

CARONDELET'S ADMINISTRATION. 1792–1797.

Who succeeded Governor Mirò?
The Baron de Carondelet.

What was Carondelet at the time of his appointment?
Governor of San Salvador in Guatemala.

Where is Guatemala? [See Map of Central America.]

What event produced, at this time, excitement in New Orleans?

The French Revolution. The French King Louis XVI had been executed, and France was now a Republic.

Why did this event excite the minds of the colonists?

Because the colony, having been originally founded by the French, had never forgotten their love for France.

What bold step was taken by some of the people?

One hundred and fifty of the citizens openly petitioned the French Republic to take Louisiana under its protection again.

Did France attend to this petition?

Not directly, but she sent agents about the Western States to try to organize an expedition to seize the colony from Spain.

Who was the principal instigator of this movement?

Genet, the French Minister to the United States.

What prevented this movement from being successful?

The determined action of General Washington, who was then President of the United States, and who declared that he would put down any attempt to attack a friendly nation like Spain.

What measures did Governor Carondelet take to repel the danger?

He built new fortifications around New Orleans.

For what important agricultural event is the year 1794 *noted?*

The first sugar was made in Louisiana in that year.

Why was this event important?

The cultivation of the sugar-cane has contributed more to the prosperity of the State than that of any other of her products.

*Was this the first time that the sugar-cane had been culti-
vated?*

No; it was first introduced in 1751; but up to 1794,
no planter had been able to make the syrup granulate,
and so convert it into sugar.

To whom is the honor of this triumph due?

To Etienne de Boré.

Who was this Etienne de Boré?

A planter, living about six miles above New Orleans.

For how much did de Boré dispose of his first crop?

He sold it to the Americans for $12,000.

*In what manner was the right of free navigation of the
Mississippi at last secured?*

By a Treaty between the United States and Spain.

When was it signed?

October 20, 1795.

What did this Treaty stipulate?

That the whole width of the river, from its source to
the sea, should be free to the people of the United
States.

What else was stipulated?

That the Americans should have the right for three
years, to use the port of New Orleans as a place of deposit for their produce; and that, after that, if Spain
did not choose to let them continue there any longer,
she should assign them some other spot.

Was Spain very willing to enter into this Treaty?

No.

Why, then, did she at last agree to it?

Because she was afraid that, if she did not do so, she
would expose herself to lose the whole province.

SPAIN, in this, preferred to give up a part rather than to lose a whole.

What was made by the Treaty the Southern boundary of the United States ?

The Natchez district, at a point 36 miles below Natchez.

What became of the Natchez district under this ?

It was transferred to the United States.

What was made the Western boundary ?

The Mississippi River. Spain retained all South of the Natchez line on the East bank, and all the vast territory lying West of the river as far as the Pacific Ocean.

How much territory on the East bank did this give the Americans ?

More than 1,800 miles, from the 31st degree of latitude (opposite the mouth of Red River) to the 42d.

When did Governor Carondelet's administration close ?

August, 1797.

To what praise is he entitled ?

To that of having done more than any of his predecessors to improve and beautify the City of New Orleans.

BARON CARONDELET deserves the credit of having been the most active of the Spanish Governors in improving New Orleans.

In 1792, he divided the city into four wards. It was during his administration, and at his recommendation, that the city was first lighted with oil lamps. To defray the expenses of these lamps and the oil, a special tax was levied upon the chimneys. The number of the chimneys once known, it was easy to determine the amount of the tax.

Just think how big a tax would that be of $1, levied upon each chimney in New Orleans in the year 1877 !

The fortifications built by Governor Carondelet, although of inferior strength, and not at all capable of sustaining any long siege, were considered as being something very strong by the people. One fort was erected where the United States Mint now stands. Another stood at the foot of Canal Street. A strong redoubt was built on Rampart Street. Others were built at each of the angles of the old City of New Orleans. Of course all signs of these have long since disappeared.

CHAPTER XXIV.

GAYOSO'S ADMINISTRATION. 1797–1799.

Who succeeded Carondelet?

Brigadier General Gayoso de Lemos, generally known as Gayoso.

What had Gayoso been before?

Spanish Commandant of the Natchez district.

What distinguished strangers reached New Orleans at this time?

The Duke of Orleans (afterwards Louis Philippe, king of the French) and his two brothers.

Why had they come to New Orleans?

Exiled from France, they came partly for pleasure, and partly to claim the hospitality of the people.

How were they received?

Costly entertainments were given to them by the principal inhabitants. They spent several weeks in the city and vicinity.

What was the principal event of Gayoso's administration?

The Americans, after many delays, were finally put into possession of the Natchez and Yazoo Districts.

4

What occurred in July 18, 1799?

The death of Governor Gayoso, aged 48 years, from a malignant fever.

CHAPTER XXV.

CASA CALVO'S ADMINISTRATION. 1799–1801.

Who was Gayoso's successor?

The Marquis of Casa Calvo, sent over from Havana by the Captain-General of Cuba.

What was the population of the old colony at that time?

About 70,000, including that of the Natchez district, which had just been transferred to the United States.

To what had this increase been owing?

To the liberal offers that had been made by Spain to all immigrants.

State the improvement that had taken place in the cultivation of sugar since 1795.

While there had been, in that year, only *one* plantation yielding sugar, there were, in 1800, *more than sixty,* producing annually more than 4,000,000 lbs. of sugar.

What power was, at this time, trying to obtain Louisiana?

France.

Who then ruled France?

The celebrated Napoleon Bonaparte, as First Consul.

What had led to the negotiations with Spain?

Napoleon had clearly seen that Louisiana, being once more in the hands of the French, would make France a formidable power in the New World.

What made Spain the more willing to cede Louisiana to France?

Her fears of the growing power of the United States. She believed that if Louisiana were in the hands of the French, she would be a rampart against any invasion of Mexico by the Americans.

When was Louisiana ceded by Spain?

October 1, 1800—by the Treaty of St. Ildefonso.

What did she bind herself to do?

To deliver to the French Republic, within six months, the colony of Louisiana as it then stood.

Did France receive all the territory which she had before ceded to Spain? If not, why?

What was there peculiar about this Treaty?

It was for a time kept secret from the world.

Why?

France was then at war with England; and she feared that, if England heard of the cession, that country would at once attack Louisiana.

What may be said of Casa Calvo's administration?

It was uneventful.

When did it close?

June 15, 1801.

CHAPTER XXVI.

SALCEDO'S ADMINISTRATION. 1801–1803.

Who succeeded Casa Calvo?

General Juan Manuel de Salcedo.

What was one of the acts done under his administration?

The right of Americans to deposit their produce at

New Orleans was suspended; and they were forbidden to trade in any part of the colony.

Who was responsible for this high-handed measure?
Morales, who was Intendant of the colony.

What effect did it produce in the West?
Universal indignation.

What did the Western States declare?
"*The Mississippi is ours by the law of nature. It is our streams and rivers that swell it and make it so mighty, and we are resolved that no power in this world shall deprive us of this right.*"

To whom did they appeal for redress?
To the President of the United States.

Who was then President of the United States?
Thomas Jefferson.

Who can tell for what great State Paper Thomas Jefferson is famous?

What did they threaten, in case that the United States did not help them?
"No Protection—No Allegiance!"

What did the President do?
He addressed the Spanish Government on the subject; demanding compliance with the Treaty.

Whom did he, at this time, send as U. S. Minister to France?
Robert R. Livingston.

What instructions did Mr. Livingston receive?
He was to find out if Spain had really made the cession to France; and above all, whether West Florida had been included in the Treaty.

What did President Jefferson hope to do, if it had not?
To buy Florida from Spain, as he dreaded so powerful a neighbor so near to Georgia and South Carolina.

When did Livingston reach France?
In December, 1801.

Did he succeed in gaining much information about Florida?
No, the French Minister was a very shrewd and wily politician who thought a great deal and said very little.

Can you tell me his name?
Prince Talleyrand.

How did Talleyrand manage to baffle Livingston?
He would put him off, month after month, by declaring that it was true that the cession had been talked of; but that nothing had been settled; and that he could not, therefore, really say whether Florida was included in it, or not.

How far was all this true?
Only so far that France, fearing what England might do in the event of another war, had not yet taken open possession of Louisiana.

How long was it before Talleyrand informed Livingston that Spain had not ceded Florida?
More than a year.

Who can tell what the western limits of Spanish Florida were?

CHAPTER XXVII.

SALCEDO'S ADMINISTRATION (CONTINUED). THE PURCHASE OF LOUISIANA BY THE UNITED STATES. 1803.

What news reached France at the beginning of 1803?
That the American Congress were about to raise 50,000 men to invade Louisiana.

Whom did the President send, at this time, as Envoy Extraordinary to France?

James Monroe.

What did James Monroe become afterwards?

Why did President Jefferson make this appointment?

To show the French Government that the United States, by sending so distinguished a man as Mr. Monroe, were in earnest.

What was Mr. Monroe instructed to do?

To offer, on the part of the United States, to buy Florida (from Spain) and the District of New Orleans (from France).

Why did the United States specially desire New Orleans and not the rest of Louisiana?

They wished to secure for the Western people a sure place of deposit for their produce, of which they could never be deprived.

What astonishing news did Monroe, on reaching Paris, receive from Mr. Livingston?

That Napoleon was willing to sell not only New Orleans, but the *whole colony of Louisiana.*

What had led Napoleon to this change of opinion?

The fact that war was about to break out again between France and England.

In what way would this have been likely to affect Louisiana?

England was threatening, in the event of war, to capture New Orleans, and hand the city over afterwards to the Americans.

What would have made it easy for England to execute this threat?

She had in the West Indies a powerful fleet, with

which she could have reached Louisiana long before the French expedition could have started from France.

Did Mr. Monroe have any instructions to buy the whole of Louisiana?

No ; but both himself and Mr. Livingston considered the offer as too important to allow them to hesitate to close with it.

What was the sum at first wanted by Napoleon?

Twenty million dollars, including the payment, by the United States, of the debt due by France to certain American citizens.

To how much did this French debt amount?

About $4,000,000.

How was this considered by Monroe and Livingston?

As being too large a sum for the United States to pay.

What sum was finally agreed upon?

Fifteen million dollars, including the debt.

When was the Treaty of Purchase signed?

At Paris, April 30, 1803.

What did Napoleon say on this occasion?

"*Let the Louisianians know that we separate ourselves from them with regret ; that we stipulate in their favor everything that they can desire ; and let them retain for us sentiments of affection.*"

Was Florida included in this sale?

That was a disputed question at this time.

How was it a disputed question?

The United States declared that Florida (West) had been sold with Louisiana. Spain was positive that it had not.

What did France say about it ?

France let Prince Talleyrand speak for her ; and Talleyrand said that he did not know.

How did the United States decide the question afterwards?

They declared, point-blank, that West Florida *was* sold, along with Louisiana.

What seems to be the true state of the case ?

That the United States came nearer the truth than the others.

CHAPTER XXVIII.

SALCEDO'S ADMINISTRATION (CONTINUED). LOUISIANA TRANSFERRED TO THE UNITED STATES. 1803.

How was the purchase of Louisiana considered ?

As being, next to the Independence of the United States, the most important measure that had been undertaken by the American Government.

What power protested against the sale of Louisiana ?

Spain.

What was the ground of this protest ?

Spain declared that France, when she had received the province, had solemnly promised never to sell or give it away.

What did Spain kindly suggest that the United States should do ?

That they should give Louisiana back to France.

How did the Americans receive this suggestion?

With ridicule. They declared that no such promise had been put into the Treaty between Spain and France ;

that the United States had bought Louisiana in good faith ; and that they meant to keep it.

How long was it before France really took possession of the colony ?

Not until November 30, 1803.

SPAIN AND FRANCE seemed to have been playing a very selfish part in this matter. They consulted their own interest. As to the Louisianians they never once thought of them.

Of course, France was bound to take formal possession of Louisiana before she could sell it to the Americans. You must own a thing before you can dispose of it to another. This is why France, on the 30th of November, 1803, received the colony from the Spanish Commissioners.

Had she done so before, England, that was waiting only to find a weak spot in her enemy, would have swooped upon New Orleans. But France was safe in receiving Louisiana openly from Spain, three years after it was hers by right of treaty, because England knew—as all the world knew—that the United States had bought Louisiana, and that not many days would pass before the Stars and the Stripes would be waving in the place of the French Tri-color.

England had no longer an excuse to attack New Orleans. France had received her $15,000,000 in cash. The United States had acquired the vast extent of territory then known as Louisiana. Both had reason to be equally well satisfied.

Only England grumbled a little, because France had not taken possession soon enough to enable her to profit by it. Spain grumbled a great deal, because France had not chosen to keep her gift.

But Spain was wrong in this. Louisiana was a gift never intended for Kings to keep.

Who was the French Commissioner to receive the colony ?

Laussat.

Who were the Spanish Commissioners to cede the colony ?

The Marquis of Casa Calvo, and Governor Salcedo.

What did Laussat say on taking possession ?

That it would not be long before Louisiana would be ceded to the United States.

4*

When did this cession to the Americans take place?
December 20, 1803.

Who were the American Commissioners?
General James Wilkinson, and W. C. C. Claiborne, who had been Governor of the Territory of Mississippi.

Who was General Wilkinson?

Under what conditions was Louisiana received into the Union?
As a territory at first, with the understanding that the inhabitants would be admitted, as soon as possible, to all the rights and privileges of American citizens.

What have you to notice about the repeated transfers of Louisiana?
That France had given the people away to Spain ; Spain to France again ; and France to the United States, without once asking them whether it would please them to be transferred, or not.

CHAPTER XXIX.

A SHORT REVIEW OF THE DOMINATIONS.

How long did the first French domination last?
About one hundred and sixty-eight years.

How long did the Spanish domination last?
Thirty-four years and a few months.

From what year to what year?

How long did the second French domination really last?
Only twenty days.

How long has the American domination lasted?

What might be said generally of the Spanish domination?
That it had made itself very popular in Louisiana.

What was the solitary stain upon it?
The execution of the French conspirators by General O'Reilly.

What had been the population of New Orleans when the Spaniards came?
Three thousand one hundred and ninety.

What was it when the Americans took possession?
About ten thousand.

What is it now?

AMERICAN DOMINATION.

CHAPTER XXX.

THE TERRITORIAL GOVERNMENT. GOV. CLAIBORNE'S ADMINISTRATION. 1803–1807.

How did the people of New Orleans look upon the cession to the United States?

The Louisianians were, for many years, opposed to it.

Of what did they complain?

That, by the Treaty with France, Louisiana should have been admitted at once as a State into the Union.

Why was not this complaint just?

Because what the Treaty had really stipulated was, not that Louisiana should be admitted *at once*, but that it should be admitted *as soon as possible* under the laws of the country.

What had Congress done in the beginning?

It had divided the new province into two parts—the "TERRITORY OF ORLEANS," and, outside of that, the DISTRICT OF LOUISIANA.

What did the Territory of Orleans include?

The city and district of New Orleans, and the greater part of what is now known as the State of Louisiana.

What answer did Congress give the people of New Orleans?

That the new Territory of Orleans should remain a

territory, like all other territories of the United States, until it had a population of 60,000 when it would be received as a State.

Did this decision please the Creoles?

Not at first. Many continued, for some years, to believe themselves unjustly treated.

Who were most active in inciting them?

The Marquis de Casa Calvo and the ex-Intendant Morales.

Do you remember anything of this Ex-Intendant Morales?

Was he a friend of the Americans?

Why had those Spanish officials remained in the colony?

Under the pretext of settling the affairs of Spain.

What foolish idea did they make a good many silly people believe?

That it would not be long before Spain would have Louisiana back again.

How did Governor Claiborne meet these reports?

With these noble words in a letter written to Casa Calvo : " *The power does not exist which can shake the authority of my country over this territory.* "

What came to make matters worse about 1805?

The prospect of a war between the United States and Spain.

What had given rise to this?

Spain claimed for herself more of the territory sold by France to the United States than she had a right to claim.

By what name was the portion claimed by Spain known?

West Florida.

What did the United States say in regard to this claim?

That West Florida was, by right, a part of what they had bought from France.

During these disputes, under what Government did West Florida remain?

That of Spain.

Where did Spain still have troops?

At Baton Rouge and Mobile.

What had made Governor Claiborne anxious?

He had a very small force of U. S. troops; and he feared that, in case of an attack by Spain upon New Orleans, the Spanish citizens would not assist him.

What precaution did he take in 1806?

He ordered Casa Calvo and Morales to leave the territory.

Did they obey him?

Yes; but not before grumbling very loudly against the order.

Why was this action of the Governor proper?

Because those men, in the case of a war with Spain, would have been dangerous to his Government.

In what year was the 4th of July celebrated for the first time in New Orleans?

In 1806.

Can you state the population of the Territory in that year?

Fifty-two thousand nine hundred and ninety-eight persons, white and black.

CHAPTER XXXI.

THE TERRITORIAL GOVERNMENT. THE CONSPIRACY OF AARON BURR. 1806–1807.

What new danger came to disturb Governor Claiborne at this time?

The famous conspiracy of Aaron Burr.

What had Aaron Burr been?

He had been a Vice-President of the United States.

What was the character of this conspiracy?

Burr had resolved to separate the Western States from the Union and to establish a new Government West of the Alleghany Mountains.

Where had Burr found most active supporters?

In Kentucky and Tennessee.

In what way did the Burr conspiracy trouble Governor Claiborne?

It was understood that Burr would attack New Orleans with a large army, and compel the people to join his proposed Government whether they wanted to do so or not.

What European power was said to be secretly assisting Burr?

Spain.

Do you know anything which would make it probable that this was true?

How was the danger finally avoided?

Burr was arrested in January, 1807, in Mississippi, before he could organize his army. He was afterwards taken to Richmond, Virginia, for trial.

What can you say of Aaron Burr?

He was a man of great talent, but a bad patriot, and a most dangerous citizen for a Republic of freemen.

CHAPTER XXXII.

THE TERRITORIAL GOVERNMENT. 1807.

What event occurred to relieve Claiborne's anxieties?

The arrival of a large number of U. S. troops, in 1809.

Who was their commander?

General Wilkinson.

What sad circumstance is recorded of these troops?

Out of nineteen hundred and fifty-three who reached New Orleans in April, seven hundred and ninety-five died before September, of a terrible epidemic.

To what was this mortality said to be largely owing?

To the quartering, by General Wilkinson, of these troops on the unhealthy lands of Terre aux Boeufs, about eight miles below the city.

What effect did this disaster have?

It raised so great an excitement against Wilkinson, that he was removed from his command by the President.

Who was ordered to succeed him?

General Wade Hampton.

GENERAL WADE HAMPTON was the father of General Wade Hampton, now Governor of South Carolina. Brave deeds and honorable lives belong to both father and son.

CHAPTER XXXIII.

THE TERRITORIAL GOVERNMENT. THE BAYOU SARANS REVOLT AGAINST SPAIN. 1810.

What occurred in the year 1810?

A revolt of the inhabitants of the town of Bayou Sara against the Spaniards.

In what province was Bayou Sara?

In that of West Florida, claimed by the United States, but still occupied by Spain.

What fort did the Bayou Sarans attack and capture?

The Spanish fort at Baton Rouge.

What had encouraged them to make this movement?

Spain was, at that time, at war with Napoleon, and could not attend to little interests in Louisiana.

What next did the insurrectionists do?

They declared West Florida independent of Spain.

What did they do after that?

They asked to be annexed to the United States, under the name of the *" State of West Florida."*

What answer did President Madison make?

He told them quietly, that the *District* of Florida already belonged, by the Treaty of 1803, to the United States.

Of what Territory did he say that it formed a part?

Of the Territory of Orleans.

Whom did the President direct to take possession of the District?

Governor Claiborne.

What did Claiborne do?

He marched at the head of militia to St. Francisville,

and, on December 7th, 1810, took possession in the name of the United States.

How did the people receive him?

They forgot all about their claims to being a State, and cheerfully submitted to his authority.

What Parishes were made out of the new District?

Feliciana, East Baton Rouge, St. Helena, St. Tammany, Biloxi and Pascagoula.

What are the Parishes of Feliciana, East Baton Rouge, St. Helena, and St. Tammany sometimes called?

The Florida Parishes.

In what State are Biloxi and Pascagoula now?

CHAPTER XXXIV.

LOUISIANA BECOMES A STATE. 1812.

What important event occurred in November, 1811?

The meeting of the Constitutional Convention.

For what purpose did the Convention meet?

To frame a Constitution, under which the Territory of Orleans was to be admitted into the Union as a State.

Why was the Territory ready for admission?

Because its population was over 60,000—the number prescribed by Congress for the admission of a State.

When was it admitted as a State?

April 30, 1812.

Who can tell of what important event was the 30th of April the ninth anniversary?

What name was given to the new State?

Louisiana.

Who was elected the first Governor of the State?

Governor Claiborne.

What did this choice show?

The great confidence of the people in Governor Claiborne's capacity and honesty.

How long had Claiborne been Territorial Governor?

As TERRITORIAL GOVERNOR, W. C. C. Claiborne had been *appointed* by the President of the United States. The Territories are the children of the Union; and the Territorial Governors are the guardians selected to watch over those children. As soon, however, as a Territory becomes a State, she then becomes the equal of all the other States. Her people then *elect* their Governor.

CHAPTER XXXV.

WAR WITH ENGLAND. 1812–1814.

What occurred in 1812?

War was declared between the United States and England—generally called the War of 1812.

How did this war affect Louisiana?

It was known, from the beginning, that England intended to attack New Orleans.

Of what did Governor Claiborne complain?

That the Government had withdrawn the United States troops from New Orleans, and left it defenceless.

Why had the Government done so?

Because no immediate danger was anticipated for Louisiana.

What did Claiborne do?

He appealed to the Government to send other troops.

Was the request attended to?

Not immediately. All the battes of the war were then being fought in the Atlantic States and on the Great Lakes. Of course, all the Government forces were needed there.

What new event made Claiborne more anxious?

The rumor that a part of the British army, intending to attack New Orleans, was actually gathering at Pensacola, Florida.

When was this?

In the spring of 1814.

What was it said that this army, if successful, would do?

That it would restore Louisiana to Spain, England's firm and faithful ally.

What did Col. Nicholls, the British commander, do to tempt the Louisianians?

He addressed a proclamation urging them to rebel against the United States.

Did this proclamation produce any effect?

It excited only ridicule and contempt.

Did Claiborne report this action of Col. Nicholls to the Government?

At once; and it forced the Government to take decisive measures.

What good news soon came to restore public confidence?

That volunteers would be sent from Tennessee and Kentucky as soon as possible.

Who was to command this army?

General Andrew Jackson, the most famous officer in the American army.

Where was General Jackson at this time?

Near Mobile, watching the movements of the British.

When did he reach New Orleans?
December 1, 1814.

What did he say to cheer the people?
That, with the army coming down from the West, and the assistance of the brave Louisianians, he would drive the English from their shores.

CHAPTER XXXVI.

THE SMUGGLERS OF BARATARIA.

During these years, what men were giving Governor Claiborne much trouble?
A band of smugglers, composed of desperate men of all nations.

Where did these smugglers have their headquarters?
On the Island of Grande Terre, in Barataria Bay.

By what name were they generally known?
The Smugglers of Barataria.

What other name was given to them?
The " Pirates of Barataria."

What gave rise to this name?
It was said that they carried the black flag, and attacked vessels of all nations.

What was their answer to this charge?
They admitted that they were smugglers, but denied that they were pirates.

What reason did they give for this?
They said that they were privateers, cruising with the permission of France, and carrying the flag of the

Republic of Carthagena, a province in New Grenada, South America, which had rebelled against Spain ?

What did they say about attacking vessels of all nations ?
They denied it, and declared that they attacked only the vessels of Spain, which was then at war both with France and Carthagena.

How many, it was said, belonged to this band ?
Between two and three hundred resolute men.

Who were their leaders ?
John and Pierre Lafitte.

Who were they ?
Two brothers, Frenchmen by birth.

Why did Governor Claiborne wish to capture them ?
Because they were engaged in a large smuggling trade, which was against the laws of the United States.

Why did not the various expeditions sent against them, at first succeed ?
The people, who could buy goods from them much more cheaply than anywhere else, sympathized with them, and always warned them when any expedition started.

Did the people believe that the Baratarians were pirates ?
No ; they thought that they were nothing more than smugglers, and, of course, many of them did not see much harm in that.

The Spanish officials never really believed that there was anything wrong in smuggling. Smuggling, therefore, was not looked upon as a serious offence by the people of New Orleans, and nothing that Governor Claiborne could do could make them think very harshly of the Baratarians.

Was their stronghold at last captured ?
Yes, in September, 1814.

What made this seem at the time a little harsh?

John Lafitte, before he knew anything of the expedition, had offered his services and those of his brother and band to Governor Claiborne, to help the Americans against the English.

Do you know of anything which renders this offer more noble?

Lafitte had previously received proposals from Col. Nicholls, at Pensacola, to join the British service.

What temptation had Col. Nicholls thrown out to him?

The rank of Captain in the British army, and the sum of $30,000.

What was Lafitte's reply?

He asked time to consider the matter; and at once wrote to Governor Claiborne.

How did Claiborne receive his offer?

Under the advice of a military council, he declined it.

Who finally accepted the services of Lafitte and his band?

General Jackson himself, who never hesitated to do what he thought was right.

How did the Lafittes return this confidence?

They and their men fought so gallantly as to receive General Jackson's thanks in a "General Order."

What do you think of the Baratarians?

Were they pirates? Or were they smugglers?

After answering this question, what else were they?

CHAPTER XXXVII.

THE BATTLE OF LAKE BORGNE. 1814.

What did General Jackson do on his arrival?

He visited all the forts, and gave orders to strengthen them.   He also established others.

What orders did he give about Bayou Manchac and other Bayous leading from the Gulf of Mexico and the lakes?

That they should all be obstructed to prevent the English from passing into the interior.

What effect did this order have so far as Bayou Manchac was concerned?

Bayou Manchac, which was formerly much used as an outlet for vessels from the Mississippi to the Lakes, has remained closed ever since.

PASSENGERS along the Jackson Railroad must have frequently noticed the dead look of this Bayou, from the bridge that spans it. Its lazy waves tell eloquently the story of the patriotic energy that, in days past, made the waters of commerce cease to flow.

How is the first battle fought between the Americans and the English, December 12, known?

As the battle of Lake Borgne.

What was the strength of the American fleet?

Five gun-boats, with twenty-three guns and one hundred and eighty-two men under Commander Thomas A. C. Jones.

Was the British force larger?

It was much larger, consisting of forty-five launches and barges, armed with forty-three guns, and manned by twelve hundred men—the whole under the command of Captain Lockyer.

Where did the fleets meet?

Near the Rigolets.

Where is the Pass of the Rigolets?

Who were the victors?

The British force was so much stronger than the American, that all the gun-boats, after hard fighting, fell into the enemy's hands.

Give a proof of how bravely the Americans had fought?

While their loss was forty-five killed and wounded, that of the British was not less than three hundred.

What was the result of this engagement?

It left the coast of Louisiana entirely defenceless.

Where was the British fleet stationed at this time?

Off Ship Island.

ALL WHO HAVE TRAVELED through Lake Borgne must have noticed the white sands of Ship Island glistening in the sun.

Ship Island is one of four low islands that, stretching ten or twelve miles along the Gulf coast, form the Mississippi Sound. It is, by no means, a large island. It is only seven miles long, and three-quarters of a mile wide. It belongs to the State of Mississippi, but is really ten miles from the nearest point of that State.

Ship Island is an imposing landmark in the history of Louisiana, as Colony, Territory and State.

In 1699, Iberville discovered it. In 1814, the British Fleet thought it a good place for their rendezvous. In 1815, it was to its white sands and its quiet harbor, that they retreated as to a place of refuge after the awful disaster on the Plains of Chalmette. In another war, it became a safe and convenient place for organization.

What precautions did General Jackson take to defend the rear of the city?

He ordered the dragoons of Feliciana and the battalion of colored men, under Major Lacoste, to that point.

5

Was there any other colored battalion in the service ?

One other, which General Jackson, who had been so much pleased with the former battalion, had, after his arrival, organized through the assistance of Savary, a colored man.

What were the majority of the members ?

Refugees from the island of St. Domingo.

Who took command of this second battalion ?

Major Daquin.

CHAPTER XXXVIII.

THE ARRIVAL OF THE TENNESSEANS. THE CAMPAIGN OF 1814–1815.

What welcome arrival took place on December 19th ?

That of General Carroll with 2,500 Tennesseans.

What additional reinforcement arrived the next day ?

One thousand two hundred riflemen from the same State, under General Coffee.

What was the principal body of Louisiana militia ?

The Planché Battalion of uniform companies, so called after its commander, Major Planché, composed of young men of the highest Creole families.

THE CREOLES have, throughout the history of their State, exhibited military qualities of a high order. Bienville gratefully recognized these in his ill-starred expedition against the Chicka- saws. Vaudreuil declared them to be the fittest men to fight with those boldest of Indian warriors. Galvez, no bad judge, was enthusiastic in their praise. The keen eye of Jackson saw their valor at Chalmette. And, in the chaparrals of Mexico, and on hotly contested fields nearer home, the Creole never lagged in the advance or fell back in the charge.

What was at this time the strength of the American army?
Between five and six thousand men, including United States regulars, Louisiana volunteers and militia, and the Tennesseans.

How strong was the British expedition against Louisiana?
It amounted to 14,450 men in three divisions.

Who was the Commander-in-chief?
General Sir Edward Packenham.

Who commanded the several divisions?
General Gibbs, the first; General Lambert, the second, and General Keane, the third.

Who commanded the British fleet?
Admirals Cochrane, Codrington and Malcolm.

Can you tell when the British forces first began collecting near Ship Island?
December 17th, 1814.

CHAPTER XXXIX.

THE BRITISH ARMY COME UP BAYOU BIENVENU. 1814.

When was the first engagement by land fought?
December 23, 1814.

Where did it take place?
On the Mississippi River, a few miles below the city, near Villeré's canal.

How had the British succeeded in reaching that point?
They had, through the treachery of some Spanish fishermen, come through Bayou Bienvenu, from the Lake.

THERE IS NO REASON to judge too harshly the conduct of the Spanish fishermen, of whom there were thirty or forty living on the left bank of the Bayou Bienvenu, almost a mile and a half from its mouth on Lake Borgne. They were Spaniards. Spain was angry with the Americans, and half disposed to go to war with them about Florida. If the Spanish fishermen were traitors to Louisiana, they thought, at least, that they were true to their own country.

The first detachment of the British army ascended Bayou Bienvenu in five barges full of men with artillery. They rowed up the bayou quickly. There was an American sergeant with his party watching for them, but their number was too small for them to venture an attack upon the enemy.

And this was the way the British succeeded in occupying the banks of the Mississippi without having to pass Fort St. Philip with their fleet. They came by the back door, not the front door, of the city.

Had not General Jackson ordered Bayou Bienvenu also to be closed?

Yes; but owing to some carelessness, the order had not been obeyed.

What would have been the result if the order had been carried out?

The British army, not being able to pass through that Bayou, would have been obliged to ascend the Mississippi River from the mouth.

What was the British force engaged in this affair?
About two thousand five hundred men.

Who made the attack?
General Jackson attacked the British.

When was this attack made?
On the night of December 23.

With what force?
About eighteen hundred men.

How long did the engagement last?
From seven to nine and a half P. M.

What was the result?

Although the British remained on the ground, the attack prevented them from advancing immediately, as they had intended, upon the city.

What prevented this attack from being completely successful?

A thick fog which arose about eight o'clock and occasioned much confusion.

Give the British loss?

It was about four hundred.

And the American loss?

Two hundred and thirteen.

How had this engagement encouraged the Americans?

It had shown them that an army of British regulars could be kept back with inferior forces of American militia.

CHAPTER XL.

THE ARRIVAL OF THE KENTUCKIANS. 1814.

Where did General Jackson intrench after the battle of December 23?

On the 24th, he fell back about two miles nearer the city.

On what day was an unsuccessful attack made in their turn by the British?

December 28.

With what loss were they repulsed?

With a loss of three hundred men.

When did the British next attack the Americans?

January 1, 1815.

Explain the character of this attack?

It was merely an artillery duel, in which, although the British had twenty-eight guns to the Americans' ten, the latter silenced their opponents.

What had been the object of the British in these two attempts?

To open a breach in the American lines, so as to be able to carry them by storm, and in that way, advance nearer to the city.

What reinforcements did the Americans receive at this time?

Two thousand five hundred Kentuckians, under the command of Major-General John Thomas Adair and Brigadier-General John Adair.

Why was this reinforcement of less use than General Jackson had hoped?

Only four hundred and fifty of the body were properly armed.

NEARLY HALF OF THESE KENTUCKIANS were in want of proper clothing. This was a signal for the humanity of Louisianians. The Legislature of the State appropriated $6,000 towards clothing them. The city and neighboring parishes gave $10,000 more. The shop-keepers of the city brought out their goods for them. And the ladies of New Orleans—never wanting when Patriotism, mated with Charity, appeals to their hearts—made their clothing for them.

CHAPTER XLI.

THE BATTLE OF NEW ORLEANS, JANUARY 8, 1815.

What did the British do after the repulse of January 1?

They continued to make formidable preparations for a decisive attack.

THE BATTLE OF NEW ORLEANS.

Of what did General Jackson become convinced on the evening of the 7th?

That they would attempt to storm the breastworks the next day (the 8th).

What troops had he to resist the assault?

Not more than 3,200 of all kinds.

Where was the remainder of his army?

Those that had arms were stationed at different points which needed defence.

Do you know the actual British force in the battle of the 8th of January?

Between six and seven thousand.

Where was the American army stationed?

On the plain of Chalmette, some four miles below the city.

Describe how their lines ran?

From the river across the plain to a short distance in the swamp—the whole line being about half a mile long.

How were they defended?

By a breastwork, with a ditch in front of it, extending the whole length, and armed with only twelve pieces of artillery.

By whom was this artillery manned?

The battery near the river was manned by the New Orleans Riflemen ; batteries No. 3 and 4, in the centre, by Lafitte's Baratarians ; and those nearest to the swamp by Flaugeac's battery, and a battery served by United States gunners.

Is it true that these breastworks were strengthened by cotton bales?

It has been said that they were, but this was a mistake. No cotton bales were used in the battle of the 8th.

When did the attack begin on the 8th?

A little after sunrise, the British began to move.

Against what point was the main attack directed?

Against the batteries nearest to the swamp.

What artillerymen worked these batteries?

By what troops were they defended?

Tennesseans and Kentuckians.

Describe the manner of the attack?

The British after giving three cheers, advanced in a close column of sixty men front. They were met by a terrible fire from the American artillery and the Western riflemen. They continued to march steadily, but after a struggle of twenty-five minutes, the column, at last, completely routed, fled to a ditch some four hundred yards from our lines.

Did their officers succeed in getting them to renew the attack?

Yes ; having been ordered by their officers to lay aside their knapsacks, they advanced for a second time.

How did this second charge result?

More disastrously than the first. General Packenham, the commander-in-chief, was killed while gallantly leading the troops. They once more broke and fled to the ditch.

Who else of the principal officers were wounded in this charge?

General Mill, the second in command, was mortally wounded, and General Keane badly.

Who took command of the British after these officers were wounded?

General Lambert.

Did the British make any other attempt?

None. They were entirely demoralized, and refused to advance for a third time.

In the meantime, what other point was being attacked?

The battery near the river, defended by the Orleans riflemen, under Captain Beale.

Was this assault successful?

Only for a moment, the British force being so much larger. Colonel Rennie, their leader, had scarcely reached the breastworks when, while uttering the words "Hurrah! the day is ours!" he was shot, falling back a corpse into the ditch below.

What influence did their leader's death have upon the British?

It so disheartened them, that, in a short time, the redoubt was retaken by the Louisianians.

Was any more fighting done after this?

No. The British army, completely panic-stricken, remained in their intrenchments.

How long had the battle of New Orleans lasted?

Scarcely more than an hour. At half past nine it was all over.

What was our loss?

Only thirteen killed and wounded.

What was that of the enemy?

At least 2,600 killed and wounded.

Where had another attack been made by the British?

One on a small American force on the other side of the river.

How did that result?

Unfavorably to the Americans, under General Morgan, who were routed and driven from the position.

5*

Did the enemy hold this position long?

No ; they left it hastily three days after the battle, recrossing the river and joining the main body.

CHAPTER XLII.

THE ENGLISH RETREAT. 1815.

Where was the British fleet stationed at this time?

Near the mouth of the river.

Why were they waiting at that point?

To be ready to ascend the river, so as to be on hand to join in the triumphal entry, which the English had boasted that they would make into New Orleans.

By what fort did a part of the fleet attempt to pass to reach their main camp at Chalmette?

By Fort St. Philip, which they bombarded for seven days, but unsuccessfully.

FORT ST. PHILIP was, and is still, situated on the bank of the Mississippi, about seventy-five miles below New Orleans, and twenty-five above the head of the pass.

Opposite to Fort St. Philip, is Fort Jackson, built afterwards. It received its name in honor of General Jackson.

What did this failure determine General Lambert, the new Commander-in-chief, to do?

Seeing that it would be very dangerous to remain without communication with his fleet, he decided, at once, to retreat with his whole army.

When did the British finally retreat from Chalmette?

On the night of the 18th January, in silence and darkness.

What trick was played to prevent the Americans from knowing that they had left ?

The British left their huts standing on the morning of the 19th. Flags were flying over them, and sentinels posted as usual.

How did the Americans find it out at last ?

By the perfect silence in the British camp, and by seeing a crow eating very close to one of the sentinels.

When the Americans entered the camp, what did they find these sentinels to be ?

Nothing but stuffed figures, dressed in British uniforms and holding muskets.

Where did the British go when they left the river ?

They encamped, for a few days, on the shores of Lake Borgne.

When did the last of the invading army leave the shores of Louisiana ?

On January 27th.

What makes the victory of the 8th of January the more glorious?

The fact that the defeated army was composed of regular troops, who had fought against the soldiers of the great Napoleon, while the victorious army were militiamen only, who had never seen service.

Can you tell me the American loss during the entire campaign?

It amounted to fifty-five killed ; eighty-five wounded ; ninety-three missing—total, three hundred and thirty-three.

CHAPTER XLIII.

PEACE DECLARED. 1815.

When did General Jackson enter New Orleans?

January 23d.

In what manner was he welcomed by the grateful citizens?

A solemn Thanksgiving was celebrated in the Cathedral. General Jackson, passing under a triumphal arch erected in Jackson Square, at the point where his statue is now raised, was crowned with laurel, by a beautiful young girl representing Louisiana. On his way to the Cathedral, flowers were strewed in his path by other girls representing the various States and Territories of the United States. He was received at the door by Abbé Dubourg who, after a complimentary address, also crowned him. The army was under arms, and the whole city was out to do homage to the hero who had saved her.

What news was received in February?

That peace had been declared between the United States and England on December 24, 1814.

What does this prove?

That the battle of New Orleans was actually fought after peace had been declared, although neither of the armies had known it.

What chivalrous act is recorded of General Jackson?

He returned to General Keane, at his request, his sword, which that officer had lost when wounded on the field.

Where were the British army and fleet waiting at this time?

In the neighborhood of Mobile, at Fort Bowyer, which they had attacked and captured.

Why were they there?

They were expecting orders from the British Government to return.

When was the Treaty of Peace finally ratified?

February 17, 1815.

On receiving this news, what did the British do?

The entire army left Mobile and sailed for home.

What notice did the United States Congress take of the victory of New Orleans?

That body passed resolutions, complimentary to the people of Louisiana, for the valor with which they had defended their soil.

To whom did President Madison extend a free and full pardon?

To the brothers Lafitte and their Baratarians, as a reward for their courage and patriotism.

When did General Jackson leave New Orleans?

At the close of March, 1815.

CHAPTER XLIV.

THE GOVERNORS OF LOUISIANA. 1816-1829.

When did Governor Claiborne's administration close?

December, 1816.

Who was elected his successor?

Major General Villeré, a distinguished Louisiana officer.

What special fact is to be noted during this term?

Louisiana, for the first and only time in her history, was declared entirely free from debt.

By whom was Governor Villeré succeeded, and when?
In 1820, by Thomas Bolling Robertson.

What can be said of the progress of Louisiana at this time?
Her growth, both in population and commerce, had been remarkable.

What had produced this wonderful prosperity?
Her becoming one of the States of the American Union.

Who succeeded Governor Robertson?
Henry Johnson.

When was Governor Johnson inaugurated?
December 24, 1824.

What distinguished Frenchman visited New Orleans in 1825?
General Lafayette.

Who was General Lafayette?

What Ex-President of the United States died in 1827?
Thomas Jefferson.

Who can tell how President Jefferson is connected with Louisiana?

What did the Legislature do to show the gratitude of Louisiana towards this great man?
It voted his heirs, whom Mr. Jefferson had left poor, the sum of $10,000.

Who was Governor Johnson's successor; and in what year?
Peter Debigny, in 1828.

Who visited New Orleans, the same year, at the invitation of the Legislature?
General Jackson.

For what purpose had General Jackson been invited?

To join in the celebration of the anniversary of the battle of New Orleans.

What anniversary was that of 1828 ?

In what way was Governor Derbigny's administration suddenly closed?

By his death, October 7th, 1829, from a fall from his carriage.

As GOVERNOR DERBIGNY had died during his term of office, Mr. A. Beauvais, as President of the Senate, assumed charge of the Government for a short time.

Mr. T. Dupre was subsequently appointed Governor, and continued as such until the original term of Governor Derbigny expired.

CHAPTER XLV.

THE GOVERNORS OF LOUISIANA. THE MEXICAN WAR.

Who, after the expiration of Derbigny's term, was elected Governor?

Alfred B. Roman.

At what were the exports of New Orleans estimated by Governor Roman?

At $36,000,000—$20,000,000 of which were the produce of Louisiana.

Whence did the remaining $16,000,000 come? Who can tell?

Who succeeded Governor Roman?

E. D. White, February 2, 1835.

For what was the year 1837 noted?

For a great financial crisis, during which all the

banks of the country, including those of Louisiana, suspended.

Who succeeded Governor White, in February, 1839?
Governor A. B. Roman, elected for a second term.

Who was Governor Roman's successor?
Alexander Mouton.

What was adopted and ratified in 1845?
A new Constitution for Louisiana.

What can you say of it?
That it did not prove very popular among the people.

Who was the first Governor under the new constitution?
Isaac Johnson (February, 1846).

What important event occurred during his administration?
The war between the United States and Mexico.

What had led to this war?
Texas, which had declared itself a separate Republic, free and independent of Mexico, to which she had formerly belonged, had become, in 1845, one of the United States.

How did Mexico receive the news of this admission?
She still claimed the Texan territory as her own, and protested against it ?

What did the United States say to this?
They asserted the right of Texas to join the Union ; and war followed.

What interest did Louisiana have in this war?
She was the nearest State to Texas. The United States called upon her, as upon others, for volunteers.

How did she respond to the call?
With the greatest enthusiasm.

What sum did the Legislature appropriate for the purpose of equipping the troops?

Nearly $300,000.

What American General were the Louisianians enabled to assist?

General Zachary Taylor, who, by their timely aid, succeeded in capturing the important city of Monterey.

From what State did General Taylor come?

He was born in Virginia, but lived in Louisiana.

AFTER HIS RETURN FROM MEXICO, General Taylor was nominated, by the Whig Party, for the Presidency of the United States. He was elected and took his seat in March, 1849. He lived about a year after becoming President.

CHAPTER XLVI.

THE GOVERNORS OF LOUISIANA. TRANSFER OF THE CAPITAL TO BATON ROUGE. 1848–1856.

What important building was finished in 1848?

The State Penitentiary, at Baton Rouge, at a cost of $400,000.

Where did the Legislature meet, for the first time, January 21, 1850?

At Baton Rouge.

Why was it that they met there?

Because, under the new Constitution, the seat of Government had been transferred from New Orleans to Baton Rouge.

In what building did the Legislature meet?

In a new State House, of a castellated style of architecture.

*What other important event occurred during Governor
Johnson's term?*

The establishment of the system of Free Public
Schools, under a special Department.

PUBLIC SCHOOLS had been established previous to this period.
But they had not been deemed sufficiently important to claim the
attention of a Department, specially chosen to administer them.
They had been, for many years, under the charge of the Secretary
of State, but had, at the last, grown far beyond that official's attention.

*Who was the first Superintendent of Public Education of
Louisiana?*

Professor Alexander Dimitry.

When did Governor Johnson's successor take his seat?

January, 1850.

Who was he?

Governor Joseph Walker.

*In what did the unpopularity of the Constitution of 1845
result?*

The forming and adoption of another Constitution.

*Who was the first Governor under the new Constitution of
1852?*

P. O. Hébert, January, 1853.

For what is the year 1853 notable?

A riot against the Spanish Consul and flag in New
Orleans.

Can you explain the causes which led to this riot?

A Cuban patriot, named Lopez, had organized in
New Orleans an expedition to seize the island of Cuba
from Spain. That expedition started from the city and
was unsuccessful.

What immediately led to it?

After the failure of the expedition, Lopez and some

of his American companions were executed by the Spaniards. This so exasperated their friends in New Orleans,
that they attacked the Spanish Consulate.

For what is the year 1853 *memorable?*

As the year of the most terrible epidemic of yellow
fever which had ever visited New Orleans.

AN EXPLANATION.

The writer, in what he has written of the Civil War, has been compelled, under the restriction which it has seemed proper for him to adopt, to leave out of the State-picture that noble army who carried her banners, without reproach, in Virginia and Tennessee. Had he attempted to tell the tale of the Louisianians, both native-born and foreign, who fought with Lee and Hood, the events of four solemn years would have dwarfed, in size, as they surely did in a grand assertion of the loftiest elements of action, the entire record of nearly two centuries.

Louisiana children read, in their large histories, the details of the proud story. They know by heart, as their children will know, the names synonymous with so much courage and so much principle. Beauregard, Bragg, Polk, Harry Hays, are household words from the Gulf to the Arkansas Line. There was a certain fitness, too, that, in FRANCIS TILLOU NICHOLLS, out of one of the bravest defenders of the honor of Louisiana in war, should have risen the chosen champion of her rights in peace.

THE CIVIL WAR.

CHAPTER XLVII.

THE CONFEDERATE STATES. 1861.

By whom was Governor Hébert succeeded?
Robert C. Wickliffe in 1856.

Who succeeded Governor Wickliffe?
Governor T. Overton Moore.

What caused anxiety at this time?
The political condition of the country.

To what was this owing?
To the suddenly developed strength of a new party called the Republican Party.

THE REPUBLICAN PARTY first started in the Northern States. Its main principle was hostility to the institution of slavery, as established in the Southern States. Its growth was slow, but towards 1858, it began to assume colossal proportions. The South feared that the success of the Republican party would endanger her own interests. When Abraham Lincoln, of Illinois, was nominated by that party for the presidency, the South was alarmed. When Mr. Lincoln was elected President, the South believed that the entire power of the United States would, at once, be exerted to abolish slavery, without regard for the rights of the owners of slaves, and, through this measure, to imperil the very existence of the States themselves. There seemed to be sufficient ground for this fear in the excited speeches of promi nent Republicans, and in the intemperate resolutions, passed by the Chicago Convention, which nominated Mr. Lincoln.

The South thought it wise to resist the movement at the outset. So it was that, after repeated endeavors to obtain a positive assurance from the triumphant party, all of which proved vain, that Slavery would not be interfered with, the Southern States resolved at last to leave a Union in which they believed that they could not enjoy their rights.

South Carolina was the first to secede Dec. 20th, 1860. Louisiana seceded January 26th, 1861.

What name did the Southern States assume in establishing a new Government?

The Confederate States of America.

Who was elected President of the new Confederacy?

Jefferson Davis, of Mississippi.

What States formed the Confederacy?

South Carolina, Mississippi, Alabama, Florida, Georgia, Louisiana, Texas, Virginia, Arkansas, North Carolina, and Tennessee.

What city was selected as its capital?

Richmond, in Virginia.

When and where did the war actually begin?

Near Charleston, in South Carolina.

In what way did the civil war open?

By a successful attack made by the Confederates on Fort Sumter, then under the command of Major Robert Anderson, of the United States Army.

CHAPTER XLVIII.

PREPARATIONS TO ATTACK NEW ORLEANS. 1862.

THE SEAT OF WAR at the beginning of the struggle, was centered in Virginia. This prominence was rendered necessary, in a military point of view, because that State was near Washington City, the capital of the Union.

Upon the first call, Louisiana troops flocked to Virginia, and remained in that State until the end of the Civil War in April, 1865.

This is a history of Louisianians in Louisiana. It is partly also a history of other Americans in Louisiana. The individuality of the State, in a certain sense, should not properly pass beyond its territory.

What was deemed of the first importance by the United States Government?

The opening, and the keeping open, of the Mississippi River.

What large city was it thought necessary to attack?

New Orleans.

When was this attack determined on?

In the spring of 1862.

Of what was the invading force composed?

Of land and naval forces.

Who commanded the land forces?

Major-General Benjamin F. Butler.

Who was placed in command of the fleet?

Flag-Officer D. G. Farragut.

CAPTAIN FARRAGUT, for his gallantry in this campaign, was promoted to the rank of Commodore.

He was born in Tennessee, and he passed his boyhood in New Orleans, where he has relatives still living.

The American Navy is full of great and brilliant names. None is more brilliant, none more justly entitled to reverence, than that of COMMODORE FARRAGUT.

THE PLAN OF ATTACK formed was that General Butler and his troops were to wait off Ship Island until Flag Officer Farragut had made his preparations to ascend the river, with his Fleet to attack the Forts.

On the 15th of April, Captain Farragut announced that he was ready. The army, at that time, numbered 15,000 troops.

The Fleet consisted of forty-seven armed vessels—of which eight were large, powerful sloops-of-war; eighteen steam gunboats; two of them ranking as sloops-of-war; and twenty-one were mortar-schooners.

The steam sloops carried from nine to twenty-eight guns.

The gun-boats carried from five to six guns each.

Total of mortars about three hundred and ten.

What were the two forts which were to be first reduced before New Orleans could be reached?

Forts Jackson and St. Philip.

Who commanded Fort Jackson?

General J. R. Duncan, with a force of 1,500 men.

Who commanded Fort St. Philip?

Colonel Higgins, with a smaller force.

THESE FORTS were not far apart. Fort Jackson was on the Western bank, thirty miles from the mouth of the river. Fort St. Philip was on the Eastern bank, a few hundred yards above. They were both well fortified and most formidable to a fleet attempting to pass them. The impression among their defenders —commanded by two skillful officers of the old United States Navy—was that they could not be successfully attacked by any force on the Federal side. Lieut. Weitzel, of the United States Engineers, and on duty in the Fleet, was of the opinion that, if the forts had been provided with a full complement of the best modern artillery, they could not have been reduced or passed by wooden ships.

CHAPTER XLIX.

THE PASSAGE OF THE FORTS.

When did the bombardment begin?

April 18, 1862.

How did it open?

By a terrible and united fire from the mortar-boats.

How did this plan succeed?

So little that, after six days of fire, the bombardment was finally given up.

What bold plan was next determined on by Flag-officer Farragut?

That of "running the forts."

What had already been done to facilitate this movement?

The iron cable, which the Confederates had stretched across the river from the front of Fort Jackson to the opposite shore, had been cut.

When was the attempt to cut this cable made?

During the night of April 21st.

What precaution was taken to distract the attention of the fort from those who were trying to cut the cable?

A heavy fire was kept up all along the line on Fort Jackson.

Was this attempt successful?

It was, and before daylight the cable was entirely cut.

When was Captain Farragut ready for running the forts?

On the evening of the 23d.

C

What was his plan of passage?

The mortar-boats were to cover the movement with the most rapid fire of which they were capable.

What was this fire intended to conceal?

The advance of the Federal fleet in the darkness.

In how many divisions was it decided that the fleet should advance?

In three divisions—the first one being under the command of Captain Farragut ; and the others to follow him along the eastern bank, and in the middle of the river.

What was the hour fixed for starting?

The signal to weigh anchor was given at two o'clock in the morning. At 3.30 A. M., the ships began their hazardous movement forward.

Did the forts become aware of this attack?

Yes, and they directed a heavy fire against the advancing ships.

What prevented the fire from the forts proving effective?

The darkness which shrouded the movements of the vessels.

Did the fire from the forts hurt the ships?

Some were seriously injured.   The *Varuna* was sunk. But the foremost continued in the darkness to press on, and had soon passed Fort St. Philip, and were in safety above it.

THIS WAS A MOST EXCITING RACE while it lasted. The brave and skillful gunners of the forts knew that the ships were passing. But they could not see clearly through the night. Many shots hit ; but the ships, directed by the strong purpose of their heroic commander, succeeded with one exception, in running by, injured a little, but not disabled.

Did the Confederates do anything with their Flotilla?

Some damage ; but the vessels were too small, with

the exception of the Manassas and the Louisiana, Confederate rams, to check any determined advance.

THE CONFEDERATE FLOTILLA consisted of fourteen or fifteen gun-boats. Most of them were our common river-steamboats, strengthened and armed a little. They were no match for the powerful vessels opposed to them.

What two Confederate rams were destroyed during this passage, and after it?
The Manassas and the Louisiana.

THE MANASSAS, after having gallantly attacked the Richmond, and pushed a fire raft upon the Hartford, Captain Farragut's own vessel, at length rushed in the darkness upon the Mississippi. These were all powerful sloops of war propelled by steam. In attacking the Mississippi, she ran on shore. Her career was ended when she could not move. She had but one gun, and that inferior. The guns of the Mississippi were of the heaviest calibre. A broadside from the Mississippi knocked away her smoke-stack. Nothing could be done with an iron ram, with her smoke-stack gone. Her men riddled and deserted her. A little while after, the Manassas drifted off. She went down the river filling with water, and towards the last on fire. It was sunrise. Her only gun went off. Then, like some great wounded animal of the deep, she gave a plunge, and was lost to the sight of friends and foes in the waters of the great river which she had tried to keep from the one in her efforts to guard it for the other.

Can you give the distance run by the Federal fleet?
From the starting place to a point above Fort St. Philip, where they were safe from its guns, about five miles.

What was the full time taken up in the passage?
One hour and thirty minutes.

IT MUST BE REMEMBERED that all this was done in great confusion. The ships that had passed anchored above Fort St. Philip. General Butler had not yet appeared. The Confederate Flag still waved over Forts Jackson and St. Philip. But it was clear that New Orleans could not hold out after the forts had been once passed.

To whom then is the honor of the capture of New Orleans to be ascribed?

To the fleet of the United States, under flag-officer Farragut.

GENERAL BUTLER never attempted to pass the forts. He gained a point above Fort St. Philip through one of the many bayous back of it leading to the river. The forts were still defiant, the Confederates still held them, when General Butler reached in safety that point, which had been gained through an awful and memorable night, by the noble Farragut. The way to New Orleans was opened to the *soldier*, because the *sailor* had opened it for him.

The forts did not surrender until Captain Farragut and his fleet had anchored before New Orleans. To have resisted longer would have been folly. They had nothing to defend when they could no longer save New Orleans.

As a proof of the strength of Forts Jackson and St. Philip, I quote from a report made by Lieutenant Weitzel:

"The navy passed the works, but did not reduce them. Fort St. Philip stands, with one or two slight exceptions, *to-day*, without a scratch. Fort Jackson was subject to a torrent of thirteen inch and eleven inch shells during a hundred and forty-four hours. It is as strong to-day as when the first shell was fired at it."

When did the Federal fleet come in front of New Orleans?
April 25th, at noon.

When did General Butler appear to take military possession of the city?
April 30th.

THE LOUISIANA was a huge vessel built upon the hull of a dry dock. She was propelled by four engines. The intention was to have armed her with sixteen heavy guns. She did not receive the armament in time for the fight.

The Louisiana was not more fortunate than her sister, the Manassas. Both belonged to that family of naval monsters, like

the famous " Merrimac," in Hampton Roads, which engaged singly
with three Federal war vessels ; and like that other famous ram,
" Tennessee " which, later on, kept at bay, for a time, the whole
Union fleet in Mobile Harbor. Not being able to defend her,
however, owing to the absence of her guns, and not wishing her
to fall into the hands of the Federals, three days after the passage
of the forts, her officers set her on fire and sent her down the river.
She ended her course by blowing up, and then floated down in
presence of the troops that lined the shore, and of the mortar-fleet
in the river, which struggled, on every side, to escape the blazing
wreck,—terrible even in its ruin.

CHAPTER L.

THE CAPTURE OF NEW ORLEANS. 1862.

*Who was the Commander-in-Chief of the Confederate
forces in Louisiana ?*

General Mansfield S. Lovell.

*When had General Lovell assumed command of the De-
partment ?*

October 18, 1861

*What event took place upon the approach towards the city
of the Federal fleet ?*

The destruction, by the Confederates, of property of
an immense value.

Why was this done ?

To prevent it from falling into the hands of the
Federals.

FIFTEEN THOUSAND BALES OF COTTON on the levee, and
twelve or fifteen cotton-ships in the river, were burned. Besides
these, fifteen or twenty steamboats were destroyed. The ram
Mississippi—a vessel that would have been more powerful even
than the Louisiana, but which was unfinished—was set on fire.
The dry docks were burned.

The confusion was awful. A black pall, even at midday, over-spread the city; and a judgment of fire seemed to have fallen upon land and water—upon friend and foe, alike.

To what was the capture of New Orleans due?

To the small number of Confederate soldiers within the city.

So LARGE A NUMBER of the men capable of bearing arms had left the city, that General Lovell found it impossible to defend it. They had responded to the appeal of General G. T. Beauregard, who was then second in command to General Albert Sydney Johnston. The Confederate forces were at Corinth, Mississippi, ready to resist the advance of the Federal forces, under General Grant, who with gun-boats and a large army, were on the Tennessee River near by. General Beauregard needed troops, and thousands of gallant Louisianians flocked to Corinth. The departure of these, of course, left General Lovell without men.

Louisianians all know General Beauregard. He still lives honored among us. He was during the Civil War not only the most distinguished general whom Louisiana gave, but one of the most brilliant leaders of the Confederate army.

CHAPTER LI.

GENERAL BRECKINRIDGE ATTACKS BATON ROUGE. 1862.

What was the first object of General Butler, after the capture of New Orleans?

To open the Mississippi River to the Federals.

What expedition was it proposed to undertake in further-ance of that object?

The expedition to ascend the river and capture Baton Rouge.

What gave importance to this town?

The fact that the United States Barracks had long been established there.

Who captured Baton Rouge?

The Federal fleet under Captain Farragut.

When did the town surrender to him?

May 28, 1862.

Who commanded the Federal land forces?

Brigadier General Thomas Williams.

Was there any defence made?

None whatever.

Why was this?

There were no Confederate troops at that point, and the inhabitants could not offer any resistance.

What did the force under General Williams number?

About 4,500, acting in conjunction with five gunboats and several transports.

Did the Confederates remain satisfied to lose Baton Rouge?

No; it was not long before they resolved to recapture it.

When was this expedition determined on?

In August, 1862.

Who commanded the Confederate forces?

General John C. Breckinridge.

Who was General Breckinridge?

One of the most distinguished citizens of Kentucky, who was, at the opening of the war, United States Senator from that State.

What position had been previously held by General Breckinridge?

That of Vice President of the United States, with President Buchanan, from 1857 to 1861. He was also the Democratic candidate for President in 1860.

With what force did General Breckinridge make the attack?

About two thousand six hundred men.

What powerful auxiliary did he hope would join him?

The famous ram " ARKANSAS."

THE ARKANSAS was one of those formidable rams built by the Confederate Government, the exploits of which have gained for them a reputation that is destined to last as long as the name of the Confederacy itself.

The Confederate Government had ordered the Arkansas to be built on the Yazoo River. She was not ready for action when the Federal fleet appeared before Vicksburg. Her commander, Captain J. N. Brown, was compelled to run a race for Vicksburg, before her machinery could be completed. On the morning of the 25th July, she steamed out of the Yazoo River. Three Federal vessels were watching for her at its mouth. The ram rushed at them. They scattered. Then began the real race, a race that was full of danger, a race through shot and shell, a race through bomb and mortar, a race through an entire fleet. Nothing could stop the Arkansas. She was equal to them all. At last, and it was a proud moment for those on board, as it was for those who watched her with beating hearts from the shore, she found herself in safety under the batteries at Vicksburg. After this, repeated efforts were made to destroy the Arkansas. All of these failed. Even the big Essex, after thundering at her with her huge guns, had to leave her. And, little by little, it came to be whispered that the Arkansas was invulnerable.

This was why General Breckinridge was very anxious that she should attack the gun-boats in front of Baton Rouge, while he advanced with his land forces upon the town from the Comite River, some distance in the rear, where he was encamped. But it was very hard work for the ram to get to Baton Rouge from Vicksburg. She could find no conveniences in Vicksburg to complete the machinery—let alone to repair damages from her many fights. But General Breckinridge was calling upon her to come. So, one day, she left for Baton Rouge. Her blacksmiths were making music with their hammers, as she left the protection of the batteries, and steamed down the river.

General Breckinridge—chafing on the banks of the Comite River—received a telegram. That telegram said : " *The Arkansas will be ready to join in your attack on Baton Rouge, at daylight, on the 5th of August.*"

On the morning of the 5th—long before it was daylight—General Breckinridge advanced from the Comite River upon the Federal army. The battle opened. The odds were heavy against the Confederates. But General Breckinridge trusted in the Arkansas. All day long he listened for the roar of her guns. He was never to hear those guns again. The Arkansas had dashed gallantly down. She was fulfilling her promise, and was already within hearing of the artillery of the Confederates—not more than five miles from the point where they were fighting against a superior force. When she had gone this far, the engineer announced that the machinery was so broken that it could not be repaired. The Federal gun-boats were drawing nearer and nearer. If the Arkansas could not move fast—it was the old story over again—she could not ram. If she could not ram, she was of no more use. So with the deepest grief, feeling it a stern reality, her officers fired and left her. She was free to go where it pleased her—her guns all shotted—her colors waving in the breeze. One by one, those guns, as the flames reached them, roared out ; and so the last race of the Arkansas was run, not only without dishonor, but with a glory that will long be remembered on the shores of the Great River.

What was the character of the attack made by the Confederates?

It was bravely made, and gallantly maintained.

How far did the impetuosity of the Confederates carry them?

Towards the close of the battle, as far as the back streets of the town.

What was the general result?

A signal victory by the land forces over the Federals.

Why could not this victory be made decisive?

Owing to the destruction of the Arkansas from which so much had been hoped.

6*

What Louisiana officer distinguished himself in this charge?

Brigadier-General Henry Watkins Allen, who was dangerously wounded.

GENERAL ALLEN originally entered the war as Colonel of the Fourth Louisiana Regiment. He had gained his promotion by repeated displays of a valor that made him the idol of his men. They trusted in him; and they cared for no danger when they were following him.

It was, at first, feared that General Allen had been mortally wounded at Baton Rouge. But it turned out, fortunately, that, although his wound cost him a broken leg, he finally recovered, through the care of a faithful physician and devoted nurses. He was not strong enough, afterward, to join in the active duties of the field; but he was still enabled to be of great service to the cause which he loved so deeply.

He was afterwards elected by the Confederates, Governor of the State of Louisiana. It was in that position that all his noble qualities of heart and mind shone out. No State in the Confederacy could boast of a truer, a braver, a juster, a more fearless, a more devoted champion of her rights than Louisiana had in those dark days. Can you wonder that the State, her men, her women, her children, loved Henry Watkins Allen?

What heavy loss did the Federals suffer during the assault?

The death of General Williams, the commander.

BRIGADIER GENERAL THOMAS WILLIAMS was high-toned, honorable in his dealings with men, and a gallant officer. The army which lost him deplored him; and the army that fought against him respected him. He was shot dead while crying, "Forward! my Indianians!" in leading a charge of an Indiana regiment.

What effect did the destruction of the Arkansas have upon General Breckinridge?

After hours of heroic fighting, seeing no sign of the ram, he was forced to give the order to retreat to the Comite.

This appeared to be the end of the battle; but what was the real end?

The retreat of the Federals, a short time after, to New Orleans.

In THEIR GENERAL PLAN to open the Mississippi, however, the Federals finally succeeded. Vicksburg, after a resistance that has made her name famous, surrendered on the 4th July, 1863. Port Hudson, after an equally gallant defence, followed on the ninth. When these fell, the campaign on the river was over. The Mississippi was open from the North to the sea.

CHAPTER LII.

THE TWO GOVERNORS OF LOUISIANA. 1864–1866.

When was General Allen inaugurated as Governor of Louisiana?

March 3d, 1864.

Who was known as the other Governor of Louisiana?

Hon. Michael Hahn.

What was the territory that recognized the authority of Governor Allen?

All of Louisiana, outside of New Orleans and the Federal lines.

What portion recognized Governor Hahn's authority?

The city of New Orleans, and the territory occupied by the Federal troops.

When did he become Governor?

February 22d, 1864.

IT MUST BE REMEMBERED that these two governments in the same State were owing to the peculiar condition of her military affairs. Mr. Hahn was a respected citizen of New Orleans, who remained faithful to the Union. He became Governor, then of that part of Louisiana which acknowledged Federal authority. Beyond that, Governor Allen's authority was supreme.

Where did Governor Hahn hold his seat of government?
In New Orleans.

Where did Governor Allen establish the Government of Louisiana?
At Shreveport.

In what Parish is Shreveport?

CHAPTER LIII.

IN SOUTH AND CENTRAL LOUISIANA. 1862–63.

Towards what section of the State did the Federals turn their attention?
Southern Louisiana.

Who came out of New Orleans with a brigade?
General Weitzel.

Who can tell anything about General Weitzel?

Where did he meet the Confederates?
At Labadieville, about fourteen miles from Thibodaux.

In what Parish are these towns?

What was the result of this battle?
Largely outnumbered, the Confederates retreated and left Weitzel in possession of the country.

Where was the next important battle?
Near Franklin, in St. Mary's Parish.

When?
April 14, 1863.

THIS BATTLE is generally known as the battle of "Bisland"—from the name of the owner of the place, upon which the Confederate forces were encamped.

Who were more numerous in this battle?
The Federals outnumbered the Confederates six to one.

What was the Confederate force?
Five thousand men of all arms.

What would that make the Federal force?
About 30,000—18,000 of whom were on land—and 12,000 sent in transports up Grand Lake, to operate in the rear of the Confederates.

Who commanded the Confederates?
General Alfred Mouton—one of the most gallant sons of Louisiana—who was to meet his death-wound later on, at Mansfield.

Who was the Federal Commander-in-Chief?
General Nathaniel P. Banks, of Massachusetts, who had succeeded General Butler in command of the Department.

What did the Confederates gain in this battle?
The praise of having acted like heroes in the face of an overpowering force.

What was the estimated loss of the Federals in this campaign?
Over 4,000 in killed and wounded.

THERE COULD BE BUT ONE result of the great disparity of numbers. The Confederates were compelled to retreat towards Alexandria.

Alexandria fell. They went as far as Natchitoches. Then they turned back—to capture Brashear City, now called Morgan

City. From that time, the Confederates continued in the stretch of country between the Atchafalaya and the Arkansas line—marching—manœuvring—fighting. The whole of these movements—not important in themselves—from May, 1863, afford a splendid evidence of the pluck and endurance on the part of the Louisianians. But there were more skirmishes than battles.

The next chapter will tell how two powerful Federal armies from South and East drew in their lines closely and more closely, until they met the Confederates in battle-array on the historic hills of Mansfield.

CHAPTER LIV.

THE RAID UP RED RIVER VALLEY. 1864.

What important expedition on the Federal side opened the war in 1864?

That against the Red River Valley.

THIS EXPEDITION up the rich Red River Valley had been a favorite project of Gen. N. P. Banks. He made his famous raid up the valley in March, 1864. He had been long preparing for it. He thought that it would be his masterpiece. He had soldiers enough. But being more of a lawyer than a soldier, his victories were not so numerous as his battles.

What was the character of this movement?

It was a plan for bringing three large bodies of Federal troops, from different directions, to concentrate at Shreveport.

What was the entire force of General Banks?

General Banks had an army of forty-five thousand men, and a navy to co-operate with his army, of sixty gun-boats and transports.

Who was his second in command?

General A. J. Smith.

How was the advance made?

General Smith landed at the mouth of Red River, and ascended it to Alexandria, which he captured.

For whom did he wait then?

For the main army under General Banks.

By what way was Banks approaching?

Up the Têche Bayou.

What did the united forces do?

They marched in the direction of Shreveport, the Confederates falling back.

How did the Confederates fall back?

Fighting at every point, skirmishing every day.

Who commanded the third division?

General Steele.

Where was General Steele marching from?

From Camden, Arkansas, moving southward.

Why was Shreveport regarded as so important?

Because it was the war-capital of Confederate Louisiana.

IT WAS BELIEVED that, if Shreveport was captured, the Confederate army would be compelled to leave Louisiana.

Who was the Confederate Commander-in-Chief?

General E. Kirby Smith.

TO MEET THESE FORMIDABLE FORCES, General Kirby Smith had an army scattered over Louisiana and Texas. This Department was very extensive. It included Louisiana, Texas and Arkansas. And the number of men whom he had to defend this big territory, was not large.

Who commanded the Confederates who were falling back before Banks' army?

General Richard Taylor.

GENERAL TAYLOR is a native of Louisiana. He is the son of the famous General Zachary Taylor, who, when the fathers of the present children of Louisiana were boys, distinguished himself in the Mexican War. The country was proud of old "Rough and Ready," and made him President.

General Dick Taylor was himself a brilliant successor, in military skill, of his eminent father.

How did General Dick Taylor like all this falling back?

He liked skirmishing far better ; but he didn't like that much either.

What did he resolve at last to do?

To take a stand, and give battle.

How many men had he at this time?

About 9,000, not more.

Where did he resolve to stop?

A quarter of a mile from Mansfield, a small town between Shreveport and Natchitoches.

In what Parish is Mansfield ?

What did he say to General Polignac, as he rode along the line before the fight?

"*Little Frenchman, I am going to fight Banks here, if he has a million of men.*"

GENERAL POLIGNAC was a brave and chivalrous Frenchman, who offered his services to the Confederate Government, and fought for it to the close of the war. He was in France a noble and a Prince. But, with his army comrades, he was General Polignac. With General Taylor, he was "little Frenchman."

Who distinguished himself in this battle?

General Mouton, who was killed during the engagement.

WE HAVE ALREADY SEEN who General Mouton was. He was a noble type of the chivalry and daring of the Creoles of this

State. Louisiana lost a son of whom she was proud—Louisianians a brother who had never failed them, and whose name is high in their love, to-day.

When was the battle of Mansfield fought?
April 8, 1864.

What was the result?
The Federals, in their turn, were routed and driven back several miles.

How far did they go back?
To Pleasant Hill, about fifteen miles from Mansfield.

What enabled them to make another stand here?
The arrival of reinforcements.

How did the battle of Pleasant Hill end?
The fight was heavy, but night fell on a "drawn battle."

If the advantage lies with an army which remains on the field, who should claim the victory here?
General Taylor, because he and his army camped on the battle-ground.

For HIGH COURAGE AND BRAVE FIGHTING, these battles of Mansfield and Pleasant Hill have not been surpassed, even on the Tennessee or the Potomac. For a small army to have remained masters of the field, after two days' fighting with a large army, is honor enough.

What became of General Steele's expedition from Arkansas?
General Kirby Smith was doing his best to stop him from going forward.

Did General Smith succeed in preventing General Steele from getting to Shreveport?
Certainly, because the Federals were soon in full retreat towards Arkansas.

What loss did General Steele suffer in his share of the campaign?

General Smith killed and captured 4,000 men ; captured ten pieces of artillery, and seized nearly 1,000 wagons.

What was the sum total of General Banks' famous raid up Red River Valley?

A disastrous failure.

WITH THE TERMINATION of General Banks' Raid, and his rapid retreat to the more southern parts of the State, the war in Louisiana may be said to have ended. No other engagements of any importance were fought after this.

The news of General Robert E. Lee's surrender at Appomatox Court House closed the war. Probably, the last organization of the Confederacy which laid down its arms was the Consolidated Eighteenth Louisiana Regiment. It surrendered at Natchitoches, June 9, 1865.

It will thus be seen that the Civil War closed later, in Louisiana than in Virginia.

AFTER THE WAR, GENERAL ALLEN went to live in Mexico. There his old wounds soon began to weaken him, and it was not many months before the hero had passed away upon a foreign soil, far from the State which he honored and the friends whom he loved.

A WORD TO THE CHILDREN OF LOUISIANA.

The Civil War closed twelve years ago. Twelve years ago, the skies were dark. To-day, the sun of Peace is smiling upon the land.

Your fathers fought a fight for principle, and fought it like heroes. There have been gloomy days since 1865. But the clouds have passed away, now. Louisiana sits to-day, among her sisters North, South, East and West, free—as free as the freest of them. She is of the Union—in the Union—with the Union. Remember, children :

It is better to have a whole Union than one broken into half.

It is better to have one great country than that country split into pieces.

It is better to see men of the same land at peace, than quarreling.

It is better to find them friends under the same flag, than to meet them wrangling under different flags.

It is better, any day, to have a bridge than a chasm.

And that bridge—do not forget—dear children of Louisiana! for all who bear the name of American, is the Constitutional Union of these States—that is, the Union under the Constitution. which keeps the States at peace with one another, and the Federal Government just towards all.

THE CITY OF NEW ORLEANS.

CHAPTER LV.

By whom was the City of New Orleans founded?

In what year was it founded?

What town had been the capital of the colony before New Orleans?

In honor of whom was New Orleans named?

In honor of the Duke of Orleans, afterwards Louis XV, King of France.

When was the Charity Hospital first established?

In 1737.

Through whose liberality?

Through that of Jean Louis, a sailor, who, on his

death-bed, left 10,000 livres (about $2,000) for the founding of a hospital free to all.

THIS ESTABLISHMENT was the original of the present immense building known as the Charity Hospital, on Common Street, which is under the charge of the Sisters of Charity. More than $50,000 are spent for the annual expenses of the building, which accommodates more than one thousand patients.

Can you tell when the Ursuline Nuns took possession of the edifice still in existence on Chartres Street, between Barracks and Hospital?

In 1730.

How long did they continue to stay there?

Until 1824, when they removed to a larger convent, three miles below the city.

To what use was it afterwards put?

After the State House was burned down, the Legislature assembled there.

What is the building now?

It is now the Archbishop's residence.

In what year was the St. Ursuline's church built?

In 1771, at the special request of the Nuns.

What disaster occurred on Good Friday, 1788?

A great fire which burned down eight hundred and fifty-six houses, among which were the Cathedral, the Town Hall, the Arsenal, the public prison, and all the stores and principal buildings.

When did another great fire take place?

Only six years afterwards, December 3, 1794.

Where did it begin, and what damage did it do?

It began on Royal street; and in three hours, destroyed two hundred and twelve of the most valuable dwellings, leaving only two stores uninjured.

What is to be observed of this fire?

That although more houses were burnt in 1788, the property destroyed in 1794 was more valuable.

When was the first regular newspaper published in New Orleans?

In 1794. It was published in French, and called *Le Moniteur de la Louisiane.*

What improvement was introduced into the city two years later?

In 1796, the city was lighted for the first time with oil lamps.

How many of these lamps were set up?

Eighty.

How had the people managed before this?

They used to go to bed early. If they went out at night, they had servants to carry lighted lanterns before them.

THESE OIL LAMPS were not put on posts as the present gas lamps. Ropes used to be fastened either to posts at the corner or to the four corner houses of a square. Swinging from these ropes in the centre of the street, was the oil-lamp. There are many now living who remember the time when oil-lamps swung from these ropes.

When did the yellow fever first make its appearance?

In the fall of 1796, when it proved very fatal.

In what year was New Orleans incorporated as a city?

In February 28, 1805.

Was this before or after the sale of Louisiana to the United States?

When did the first legislature of Louisiana meet?

November 4, 1805.

Was Louisiana a territory or State in 1805?

When did the first steamboat arrive from the West?
January 10, 1812.

How did the people of New Orleans welcome the steamboat?
They were greatly excited. The whole population thronged to the levee to look at the wonderful steam-vessel—the first which they had ever seen.

Who was one of the most useful benefactors to New Orleans?
Don Andres Almonaster, a Spanish gentleman.

What buildings did he erect between 1770 and 1780?
He built a larger Charity Hospital, a Town Hall, and the Cathedral, which was pulled down to make way for the present one.

DON ANDRES ALMONASTER received from the town in 1770 the large space of ground on St. Peter's and St. Ann's Streets on perpetual yearly rent. The property is still owned by his daughter the Baroness of Pontalba (or her descendants) who built those rows facing Jackson Square known as the Pontalba Buildings. The remains of Don Andres Almonaster lie buried under the Cathedral pavement, near the altar, where his name may still be seen cut into the stone. At stated times, chimes are rung in honor of his memory by the Cathedral bells.

What are the two most famous statues in the city?
The equestrian statue of GENERAL ANDREW JACKSON, on Jackson Square ; and the CLAY statue on Canal Street.

Who can tell why New Orleans should honor the memory of Andrew Jackson ?

Who can say why the site of the Jackson Monument is appropriate ?

In whose honor was the Clay statue erected?
In that of HENRY CLAY.

Who was Henry Clay?
A distinguished American orator and statesman.

THERE IS also a statue of BENJAMIN FRANKLIN in Lafayette Square. It is the work of the celebrated American sculptor, POWERS—but not a very good specimen of his art.

In the Greenwood Cemetery, a Monument has been raised to the memory of the heroic CONFEDERATE DEAD. The base of the Monument is surmounted by the figure of an armed soldier. The design is chaste ; and the sad surroundings lend an awful solemnity to that warrior in stone.

What new Monument will soon be raised ?

One to the memory of GENERAL ROBERT E. LEE.

Who was General Lee?

The beloved leader of the Confederate army in Virginia.

THE PLACE SELECTED for this Monument is Tivoli Circle. It is proposed to raise upon a mound, fifty feet high, an equestrian statue of the noble Virginian.

Name the principal squares of the city ?

Jackson Square, Lafayette Square, *Place d'Armes,* Washington Square, Annunciation, Tivoli Circle, and Coliseum Place.

Who among you, children, can give the position of all these squares?

THE JACKSON SQUARE (formerly known as the *Place d'Armes,* or place for the review of the troops) is very foreign looking. The busy river, with the thousand masts of its shipping, is in front. Across the square is the solemn Cathedral ; and on each side of that, are the quaint court houses, which take the mind back to the old Spanish colonial days. On either side of the square, are the Pontalba buildings, which although new have somehow, an old, old look about them. But it is the beauty of the venerable square itself—its rare tropical flowers and its well-kept walks— which most excite the curiosity of the strangers who come from every part of the country ; while the bronze figure of the savior of New Orleans makes it precious to the hearts of all Louisianians.

In what great organization may New Orleans take pride?
In its splendid Fire Department.

Why do you say this?
Because, from the high character of the firemen—their unselfish zeal in the discharge of their duties—and their fearlessness in the hour of danger, the New Orleans Fire Department has no equal in the country.

Who can tell what day is the " Firemen's Day ? "
For what else is New Orleans noted?
For its system of street-cars.

How is this street-car system worthy of notice?
The cars are said to be prettier, cleaner and more comfortable than those of any other city.

When was the first street-car line, under the present system established?
In 1860.

Had there been any other lines before this?
Yes, one as early as 1833.

Between what points was this line established?
Between New Orleans and Carrolton.

THE CHILDREN of the present day cannot know that this was really the *first* line of horse railroads built in the United States. The cars used then were two-storied. In the hot summers, when the sun was pouring down upon the city, this upper story, (with a canvas cover) which had to be reached by a staircase, was very pleasant.

It was not until 1866 that the old two-storied cars gave way to the present line. Many think that there were more life and more excitement about the double story. As they remember it, the breezes were cooler and fresher aloft, than in the close cars of this day.

Can you mention anything else for which New Orleans is known?
For its handsome churches and its various charitable institutions.

7

AMONG THE POINTS OF INTEREST to a stranger is the space occupied by the churches of St. Alphonsus, St. Mary and Notre Dame—three of the finest and most imposing in the city—with their adjoining school-houses and asylums. This space may be justly called the ECCLESIASTICAL SQUARE of New Orleans.

Of what famous hotel can the city boast?

The St. Charles Hotel.

Why is this hotel famous?

On account of its great harmony of proportion and its admirable portico, the most imposing in the country.

What three important buildings belong to the United States?

The Custom House, the U. S. Mint, and the Barracks.

THE CUSTOM HOUSE is probably the largest building of the kind in the country. It contains the City Post Office. THE MINT is a landmark on Esplanade Street, and fronts on the river. The Barracks are situated in the suburbs below the city, and also front the river.

For what have the people of New Orleans always been preëminent?

For their exquisite musical taste.

How has this taste been proved?

By the fact that New Orleans is the only American city where the *"Grand Opera"* has a home.

THE PEOPLE OF NEW ORLEANS, and especially the Creoles, are artists in their conception of what good music is. They are everywhere recognized as excellent judges.

What is looked upon as one of the curiosities of the city?

The "French Market."

Can you tell why this Market is called the French Market?

Because the present building is on the site of the first market built by the French founders of the city.

EVERY STRANGER GOES TO SEE THE FRENCH MARKET. Under its three roofs, every language is spoken. The buyers and sellers are men of all races. There are three buildings, each under a special roof. They are known as the "Meat Market," the "Vegetable Market," and the "Fish Market." Around these various markets, is a fringe of coffee-stands and fruit-stalls. Sometimes, the stranger sees some beings only half-civilized. The moment that he catches the smell of dried *sassafras* leaves, which make a splendid *gombo* for the well, and that of the fragrant *tisane*, which makes soothing tea for the sick ; and that he casts his eye upon the odd looking moccasin shoes, so gayly set in row with embroidered beads, then he will begin to believe that some strange people are about. But when the same person sees around those peculiar goods, women with swarthy skins and long, splendid flowing hair, and, particularly, if he should see the queer little *papooses* rolled up in some rough shawl·or rougher blanket, and laid down upon the ground, there to sleep or play as it may suit them, then he will be *sure* that these quiet, patient, dark-skinned women are INDIANS. And, perhaps, the tender thought, a thought as full of pity as it is of tenderness, will come to such strangers that those poor, lonely, houseless people are descendants of those who once were owners of the very soil on which the proud city of New Orleans now stands.

Who of the class can give the name of the Indian Village which once occupied the site of New Orleans ?

How many additions have been lately made to the city without changing the names of the places added?

Two.

Can you name one of these?

The town of CARROLTON, above the city, on the same bank of the Mississippi River.

What has Carrolton become?

The Seventh District.

Can you name the other ?

The town of Algiers, lying opposite the city.

By what number of District is Algiers known ?
By the name of the Fifth District.

What may Algiers be called ?
The " Dock City."

Why ?
Because of the number of " dry docks " there.

What is a " dry dock ? "
A dock for the use of ship-carpenters.

What do ship-carpenters do in these docks ?
Repair the shipping, and the steamboats.

Can you name some of the principal docks ?
The " Ocean Dock " ; the " Marine Dock " ; the " Vallette Dock," and the " Good Intent Dock."

ALGIERS is not a large city ; but her docks keep several hundred men busy ; and the music of the ship-carpenter's hammer is always heard in Algiers.

Can you name two places near the city on the lake shore ?
Milneburg and the New Lake End.

On what lake are these places situated ?

In whose honor is the lake itself named ?

Can you tell the origin of the name of the New Lake End ?
It is the newer settlement on the lake shore—that is, it is the settlement last established.

Which is the first established ?
Milneburg.

MILNEBURG is already an old town. It is named in honor of Milne—once a well-known citizen of New Orleans. It is reached by the Pontchartrain Railroad.

How is the New Lake End reached from the city ?
By the " Dummy " Railroad on Canal Street.

What is the real importance of this settlement?
It is built at the outlet of the New Basin.

Who of the class can tell the name of the founder of the "Old Basin"? Was he a French Governor, or a Spanish?

What is the most noticeable feature at the New Lake?
The "Lake Protection Levee."

What is the other name of this "Levee"?
"The Revetment Levee."

Why has this levee been built?
As a protection against the action of the lake.

THE GREAT EQUINOCTIAL GALE of 1877—(September 19 and 20) committed fearful ravages along the Gulf coast. Among important works destroyed was the "Revetment Levee." This is a great loss; but it is one that will be repaired, sooner or later.

CHRONOLOGICAL TABLE OF THE GOV-
ERNORS OF LOUISIANA.

I.

FRENCH GOVERNORS.

Sauvolle.........................1699-1701. Died in office
Bienville (*1st term*)...............1701-1713. Recalled
De Muys, *never reached Louisiana ;*
    died in Havana.............. 1701.
Cadillac ....1713-1717. Recalled
De L'Epinay........................1717-1718.   "
Bienville (*2d term*)..............1718-1724.   "
Périer.............................1724-1733.   "
Bienville (*3d term*)..............1733-1744.   "
De Vaudreuil.......................1744-1753.   "
Kerlerec...........................1753-1763.   "
D'Abbadie..........................1763-1765. Died in office
Aubry..............................1765-1766. Ulloa arrives

II.

SPANISH GOVERNORS.

Ulloa......................... 1766-1768. Expelled
Aubry (after Ulloa's expulsion) 1768-1769. O'Reilly arrives
O'Reilly .... 1769-1770. Returns to Spain
Unzaga........................ 1770-1777. Transferred to Caraccas
Galvez........................ 1777-1785. Made Viceroy of Mexico
Miró .... 1785-1792. Recalled
Carondelet .... 1792-1797.   "
Gayoso .... 1797-1799. Died
Casa Calvo.................... 1799-1801. Recalled
Salcedo....................... 1801-1803. Close of Spanish Domi-
                                          nation.

III.

AMERICAN GOVERNORS.

W. C. C. Claiborne *appointed Terri-*
torial Governor..................1804–1812.

W. C. C. Claiborne *elected Governor of*
State ....1812–1816.   Died in office
James Villere.......................1816–1820.   Term expired
Thos. B. Robertson ....1820–1824.   Resigned
H. S. Thibodaux (*to fill unexpired term*).........
Henry Johnson.....................1824–1829.   Term expired
Peter Derbigny.........................1829.   Died in office
A. Beauvais ⎰
Jaques Dupre ⎱ *to fill unexpired term*...........
A. B. Roman.......................1831–1835.   Term expired
Edward D. White..................1835–1839.   "   "
A. B. Roman.......................1839–1843.   "   "
Alexander Mouton..................1843–1846.   "   "
Isaac Johnson ....1846–1850.   "   "
Joseph Walker......... ....1850–1853.   "   "
Paul O. Hébert ....1853–1856.   "   "
Robert C. Wickliffe. ....1856–1860.   "   "
Thos. Overton Moore (to May).......1860–1862.   Occupation of
Brig.-Gen. G. F. Shepley, *Military*
   Governor. May ....1862.   New Orleans
Gen. Henry W. Allen, Confederate, *elected* 1864.
Michael Hahn...........*elected*, Feb. 22, 1864.
   Military Governor until March 4, 1865.
J. Madison Wells, *elected*..................1865.
B. F. Flanders.........*appointed* June 6, 1867.
Joshua Baker.............*appointed* Dec. 1867.
H. C. Warmoth, *elected*........... ...1869–1873.
John McEnery, *de jure* ⎰ ....1873–1877.
Wm. P. Kellogg, *de facto* ⎱
Francis T. Nicholls, *elected.* .... 1877.

PART II

GEOGRAPHY.

CHAPTER I.

What is Geography ?

What is Louisiana ?

It is classed as one of the Gulf States.

THE GULF STATES are those which border on the Gulf of Mexico. Such being the case, who can tell what are the Gulf States besides Louisiana ?

How is it situated?

Louisiana lies between parallels 28°, 50′ and 33° north latitude, and is included between the meridian 88° 40′ and 94° 10′ W. from Greenwich.

What may be said of Louisiana ?

It is, with the exception of Florida and Texas, the most southern of the United States.

What is its total land area ?

It has a total area of 40,790 square miles.

What is its water area ?

Two thousand three hundred and twenty-eight square miles, making a total, of land and water, of 43,018 square miles.

How many acres are included in 40,790 square miles?

Twenty-six million, one hundred and five thousand, six hundred acres.

How many acres, therefore, does this give to a square mile?

Can you tell how Louisiana is bounded?

On the north, by Arkansas along parallel 33° and by Mississippi along parallel 31°; on the east, by the Mississippi and the Gulf of Mexico; on the south, by the Gulf of Mexico; and on the west, by Texas.

What two rivers form the boundary line on the east?

The Mississippi and Pearl Rivers.

What river forms, for more than two-thirds of the distance, its boundary on the west?

Sabine River.

What is its total population by the official census taken in 1870?

Seven hundred and twenty-six thousand, two hundred and seventy-six, of whom 362,651 were white, and 364,210 colored.

What does Louisiana measure at its widest part?

Two hundred and ninety miles.

What from North to South.

Two hundred miles.

What is the capital of Louisiana?

New Orleans.

THE SEAT OF GOVERNMENT was changed in 1850 from New Orleans to Baton Rouge; and continued there until the opening of the Civil War. During the war, Shreveport became the Confederate State Capital. After the war, New Orleans once more became the seat of government.

The State Government is now administered at the State House, formerly the St. Louis Hotel, on St. Louis Street.

CHAPTER II.

THE PARISHES AND THEIR SUB-DIVISIONS.

Into what is the State of Louisiana politically divided?

Into Parishes.

With what do these parishes correspond in other States?

With Counties.

EVERY STATE IN THE UNITED STATES, with two exceptions, is divided into counties. The two exceptions are Louisiana and South Carolina. Louisiana, as we have seen, is divided into parishes. South Carolina is divided into districts.

How many parishes are there in the State?

Fifty-eight.

Name them alphabetically.

Ascension, Assumption, Avoyelles, Bienville, Bossier, Caddo, Calcasieu, Caldwell, Cameron, Catahoula, Claiborne, Concordia, De Soto, East Baton Rouge, East Carroll, East Feliciana, Franklin, Grant, Iberia, Iberville, Jackson, Jefferson, Lafayette, Lafourche, Lincoln, Livingston, Madison, Morehouse, Natchitoches, Orleans, Ouachita, Plaquemines, Pointe Coupée, Rapides, Richland, Red River, Sabine, St. Bernard, St. Charles, St. Helena, St. James, St. John Baptist, St. Landry, St. Martin, St. Mary, St. Tammany, Tangipahoa, Tensas, Terrebonne, Union, Vermilion, Vernon, Washington, West Baton Rouge, West Carroll, West Feliciana, Webster, Winn.

Into how many great classes are these parishes sub-divided?

Into five.

How are these classes known?

As the ALLUVIAL PARISHES ; the SEA MARSH PARISHES ; the PRAIRIE PARISHES ; the PINEY WOOD PARISHES ; and the GOOD UPLAND PARISHES.

THE PARISHES OF THE STATE do not always fall entirely under one class. That would be simply impossible. Some parishes belong, in the very nature of their lands, etc., to one or more classes at the same time. By this, it is intended merely to give the prominent natural divisions into which the State is classified. The parishes mentioned are mainly, or wholly, of the character given to them.

Name the Alluvial Parishes.

Ascension, Assumption, Avoyelles, Carroll, Concordia, Iberville, Madison, Pointe Coupée, St. James, St. John Baptist, St. Charles, Tensas and West Baton Rouge.

Name the Sea-Marsh Parishes.

Cameron, Lafourche, Jefferson, Orleans, Plaquemines, St. Bernard, St. Mary, Terrebonne and Vermilion.

Name the Prairie Parishes.

Opelousas and St. Landry.

Name the Piney Woods Parishes.

Calcasieu, Catahoula, Grant, Natchitoches, Rapides, Vernon, and Winn, *West* of the Mississippi ; and Livingston, St. Helena, St. Tammany, Tangipahoa and Washington, *East* of that river.   .

Where do the Good Upland Parishes mostly lie?
In North Louisiana.

Name them.

Bienville, Bossier, Caddo, Claiborne, De Soto, Jackson, Morehouse, Ouachita, Red River, Sabine, Union, Webster, and a small part of Caldwell.

THERE ARE ALSO "Good Uplands" in the "Florida Parishes," West of the Mississippi.

Who can tell what parishes are those known as the Florida Parishes?

What parishes are called the "Attakapas Parishes"?

Iberia, Lafayette, St. Martin, St. Mary, and Vermilion.

QUESTIONS ON THE MAP.

In what section of the State are the Alluvial Parishes?
In what section are the Sea-Marsh Parishes?
In what section are the Prairie Parishes?
In what section are the Piney Woods Parishes?
In what section are the Upland Parishes?

What are the most northern parishes? On what State-Line do all these parishes border? What are the most southern parishes? Which is the most western of these? Which is the most eastern? On what body of water do they lie?

Which is the most south-eastern parish? What great river empties through it into the Gulf?

What parishes border on the Mississippi State Line? Which is the most eastern of these? Which the most western? Which extends the farthest south?

Which parishes border on the Sabine River? Which on the Texas State-Line? Which parish borders partly on the Sabine River, and partly on the Texas Line?

Which parishes border on the west bank of the Mississippi River? Which on the eastern? Which parish is opposite New Orleans? Which parishes lie both on the east and west banks of the Mississippi River? Which parish has the longest front on that river? Which parish on the Mississippi River extends farthest east? What parish north of the Mississippi State Line extends farthest east? What city in Mississippi is opposite its most eastern point? What town in that parish is nearly opposite Vicksburg?

CHAPTER III.

THE ALLUVIAL PARISHES.

Name the Alluvial Parishes.

What are Alluvial Parishes?

Those which contain alluvial or bottom lands within their borders.

What are known as alluvial lands?

Lands which lie along the banks of rivers and bayous.

Into how many classes are these lands divided?

Into two classes,—arable alluvial lands (that is, lands which are fit for cultivation), and wooded alluvial lands.

What is the character of the arable lands of Louisiana?

They are said to be the most fertile in the world.

Along what river do most of them lie?

The Mississippi River.

Name some of the other principal rivers with alluvial lands.

The Ouachita, Black, Little and Red Rivers.

THESE LANDS have been formed gradually from deposits, left by the sediment brought down the Mississippi and other rivers. It has taken ages to make them what they are. They are always highest on the banks of the streams, from which they slope off into the wooded lands, which are nothing but swamps. The planters call the lands upon the streams " front lands," and those farthest from them " back lands."

There are 3,615,000 acres of arable, and 2,752,000 acres of wooded, alluvial lands in the State.

What can you say of the population which inhabits this section?

It is mainly Creole, (that is, composed of those descended from the old French and Spanish settlers) and embraces most of the oldest families in the State. There is also a very large proportion of "American" families, that is, families who came from other States to settle here.

THE POPULATION of these Parishes has always been distinguished for its courtesy and high toned hospitality. No population in the whole country is more refined than the Creole.

Which of the Alluvial Parishes derive their names from Indian tribes living on the soil at the time of settlement?
Avoyelles and Tensas.

From whom is Iberville Parish named? Madison?

What is the literal translation of the name Baton Rouge?
Red Stick.

Can you tell how the name happened to be first given?
The bark of the cypress trees—of which there were a great number on the spot at the time it was first visited —is of a reddish hue. On observing this, one of the party exclaimed "Wouldn't that tree make a fine red stick!" (*baton rouge*) ; and the name was at once given to the place.

TWO PARISHES bear the name Baton Rouge. One, on the west bank of the Mississippi River, is called West Baton Rouge—that on the eastern bank, East Baton Rouge. The city of Baton Rouge, which is on the eastern bank, contains the State Penitentiary, the Lunatic Asylum and the United States Barracks. It was for many years the capital of the State.

Why is Concordia Parish so called?
It was named in honor of the peace which, after many years of warfare, had been made between the Americans and Spaniards in that section.

THIS OCCURRED in 1795. The concord thus established pleased

both parties. "Let us call the Parish '*Concordia*,'" they said. And so it was done.

The village, containing then but a few houses, was called *Vidalia*, as a tribute of respect to *Vidal*, the Spanish commander.

Who were the first settlers of the Parishes of St. Charles and St. John the Baptist?

Two hundred German colonists who came from Alsatia, in 1720.

What was this coast for a long time called?

The German Coast.

What other name was sometimes given to it?

The "Golden Coast," from the extreme richness of its soil.

THESE GERMANS had originally been sent by John Law, Director of the Mississippi Company, to settle on his Arkansas lands But, after Law's disgrace, they abandoned Arkansas and settled in St. Charles and St. John the Baptist.

QUESTIONS ON THE MAP.

Which is the most northern alluvial parish? On what river does it lie? Opposite what county in Mississippi is it? (Issaquena County.)

Which is the most western? Which is the most southern? Which is the most eastern? What alluvial parishes border on the Mississippi? Through which parishes does Ouachita River flow? Where does it empty? Through which does Black River flow? Where does it empty? Little River? Red River? In what State does Red River rise? (Texas.) *Through what parishes does its course run? Into what river does it empty? Through what parish does it empty into that river?*

What large bayou starts from the Mississippi River in Ascension Parish, and, passing through Assumption and Lafourche Parishes empties, near Bay Marchant, into the Gulf of Mexico?

Bound Ascension Parish. Bound Assumption. Bound Avoyelles. How is Carroll bounded? Concordia? Iberville? Madison? Pointe Coupeé? St. James? St. John Baptist? St. Charles? Tensas? West Baton Rouge? East Baton Rouge? On what two lakes does St. John the Baptist border? What does St. John the Baptist Parish form?

Name the chief towns in each.

Name the most important towns in Louisiana, along the banks of the Mississippi River from the Arkansas line to its mouth.

———————————

CHAPTER IV.

THE SEA MARSH PARISHES.

Name the Sea Marsh Parishes.

What are the Sea Marsh Parishes?

Those in which sea-marsh forms, more or less, a part of their surface.

Where are most of these parishes?

They border on the Gulf of Mexico from Pearl River to the Sabine.

How far does the coast marsh extend into the interior?

To a depth varying from ten to thirty miles from the water-line of the Gulf.

In what parish does it extend the farthest back?

It extends so far back in Lafourche Parish as to pass entirely through it into St. James Parish.

What is the general character of this sea marsh?

It is low; subject to tidal overflow; filled with lakes; and crossed by numerous bayous.

What results from this?

That the coast-marsh is generally impassable.

THERE ARE TWO DIVISIONS of the coast-line. The first or eastern division lies between Cat Island, near the mouth of Pearl River and Atchafalaya Bayou, which are the eastern and western points of the Mississippi Delta. The second section extends from Vermilion Bay to Sabine Lake.

How is the eastern division of sea-marsh diversified?

By numerous islands lying in the marsh, some of which are of considerable extent.

Name some of the more cultivated of these islands?

Pecan Island, Little and Grande Chenières, Chenière-au-Tigre, and the Buck Ridges of Cameron and Vermilion.

By what else is this division diversified?

By numerous bays.

Name the bays.

Elio Bay, Barataria Bay, Timbalier Bay, Terrebonne Bay, Caillou Bay, Four-League Bay, Atchafalaya Bay, Bay of St. Bernard, Cote Blanche Bay and Vermilion Bay.

State the character of the western section of the coast-line?

It is a nearly straight beach, and has neither bays indenting it nor islands lying in front of it.

What can you say of the bayous flowing into the Gulf?

Except at their mouths, which are always obstructed by sand bars, they are deep.

What is to be said of the population of the Sea Marsh parishes?

Outside of the planters who live along the bayous, the population is very small, consisting mostly of hunters and fishermen.

QUESTIONS ON THE MAP.

*Which is the most eastern of the Sea Marsh Parishes?
Which extends farthest south? Which is the most western?
Which extends farthest north? Which contains the mouth of
the Mississippi River? Which includes the largest city?
Which contains the greatest number of bays? On what two
lakes does Orleans Parish border? Which is the most southern of these lakes?*

*Bound Cameron Parish. How is Lafourche Parish bound-
ed? Jefferson? Orleans? Plaquemines? St. Bernard?
Terrebonne?*

Name the chief towns in each.

What town is opposite New Orleans, in Jefferson Parish?
Gretna.

ALGIERS on the same bank, embraces now the Fifth District
of New Orleans.

CHAPTER V.

THE ATTAKAPAS PARISHES.

THE ACADIANS. Off the east coast of the State of Maine there
is an island formerly known as Acadie—now called Nova Scotia.
More than a hundred years ago, Acadie was inhabited by a pious,
thrifty and happy population. The island had long been the sub
ject of dispute between the French and English. It had been
settled by the French. At last, the English, proving the stronger,
seized the entire island.

This was followed by a terrible persecution of the simple
Acadians. Many of them were slain and their property was confiscated. Two hundred and fifty-three homes were burnt down
by the English, at one time. In 1756, about six hundred and fifty
of this unhappy people came to Louisiana. They hoped to find,
among their countrymen on the banks of the Mississippi, an asylum where they could enjoy their homes and rear their families

in peace. Others soon followed them. They were received in New Orleans with tenderness. Every house opened its doors to them. Governor Kerlerec gave a tract of land and farming utensils to each family.

The Acadians, for the most part, settled in the Attakapas country. There, their descendants are still to be found—as simple, thrifty and happy a population as that which, so long ago, were driven, harmless and broken-hearted from the shores of Nova Scotia.

When Governor Galvez, in 1779 and 1780, called for volunteers against the English, none offered their services more eagerly, or fought more resolutely, than the descendants of the Acadians. (See History, Chap. XIX.) The sons could not forget the wrongs of their fathers, nor the tears of their mothers.

What parishes are known as the Attakapas Parishes?

In what section of Louisiana are they?

Which of the Attakapas Parishes are Sea-Marsh Parishes also?

From what is the name Attakapas derived?

From that of a tribe of Indians that once inhabited the country.

Which is the largest of the Attakapas Parishes?

Vermilion.

Which is the smallest?

Lafayette, it being only nineteen miles long.

What river flows through Lafayette Parish into Vermilion Parish?

The Vermilion River.

What vast prairies extend on each side of the Vermilion River?

The Opelousas and Attakapas Prairies.

What picturesque hills are found in Lafayette Parish?

The Cote Gelée Hills.

For what is St. Martin Parish noted?

For possessing the finest timber in the State.

What famous bayou flows through St. Martin and Iberia, and St. Mary Parishes?

Bayou Têche.

How are the lands lying along Bayou Têche known?

As the Valley of Têche.

What makes the Valley of Têche so famous?

The extreme beauty of its scenery, and the great fertility of its lands.

Where is the most beautiful scenery on Bayou Têche to be found?

Between the towns of St. Martinsville and New Iberia.

What is the character of the Bayou below the latter point?

It is broader and deeper than it is above, and there are many large and handsome residences on its banks.

THE BANKS OF THE TECHE are quite high. They average about eighteen feet above the water, although they reach nearly twenty feet at St. Martinsville, and at Breaux Bridge, twenty-two feet. The Têche is navigable for small steamers, about six months in the year. In the summer, it is rarely more than three feet deep, and about sixty feet broad. The branches of trees often hang so low over the water, that they brush the wheels of the steamboats as they pass.

What do its inhabitants proudly call the Têche country?

The " Garden of Louisiana."

By what distinguished American poet has it also been complimented?

Henry Wadsworth Longfellow.

MR. LONGFELLOW is from Massachusetts. He is the greatest of American poets.

In what way did Professor Longfellow praise our lovely Têche?

By a beautiful poem which he wrote, called " Evangeline, A Tale of Acadie."

EVANGELINE is the gentle heroine of this poem. She was born in Acadie ; but she leaves her native country to come to Louisiana in search of her lover Gabriel, who had gone with his father to settle in Opelousas. She goes in company with her guide, the good Father Felician. They come down the Mississippi and, leaving it, pass through Bayou Plaquemine into Grande Lake, and that net work of bayous that lead to Bayou Têche. At length, Evangeline reaches Opelousas, but only to find Gabriel gone.

Speaking of the Têche country, Longfellow says :

> " Beautiful is the land with its prairies and forests of fruit trees,
> Under the feet a garden of flowers, and the bluest of heavens
> Bending above, and resting its dome on the walls of the forest,
> They who dwell there have named it the Eden of Louisiana."

What peculiarity is to be observed of Iberia and St. Mary Parishes?

These parishes contain five islands of firm bluff land, which rise mountain-like above the vast sea-marsh.

No SIGHT can be more welcome to the weary traveler, crossing the long and monotonous stretch of marsh, than that of these islands, as remarkable as they are quaint and beautiful. And, when the sun shines upon the waving grasses of the one, and the highlands and green trees of the other, no sight can be more picturesque.

What can you say of the land of these islands?

It is generally very rich.

Name them going from West to East.

Miller's Island, Petite Anse, Grande Cote, Cote Blanche, and Belle Island.

MILLER'S ISLAND is now called "Orange Island," on account of its great yield of oranges. It lies south of Lake Peigneur, and in a curve which has the shape of a new moon.

THE LARGEST OF THESE ISLANDS, Grande Cote, is not more than two miles across.

Which is the chief of these islands?

Petite Anse Island.

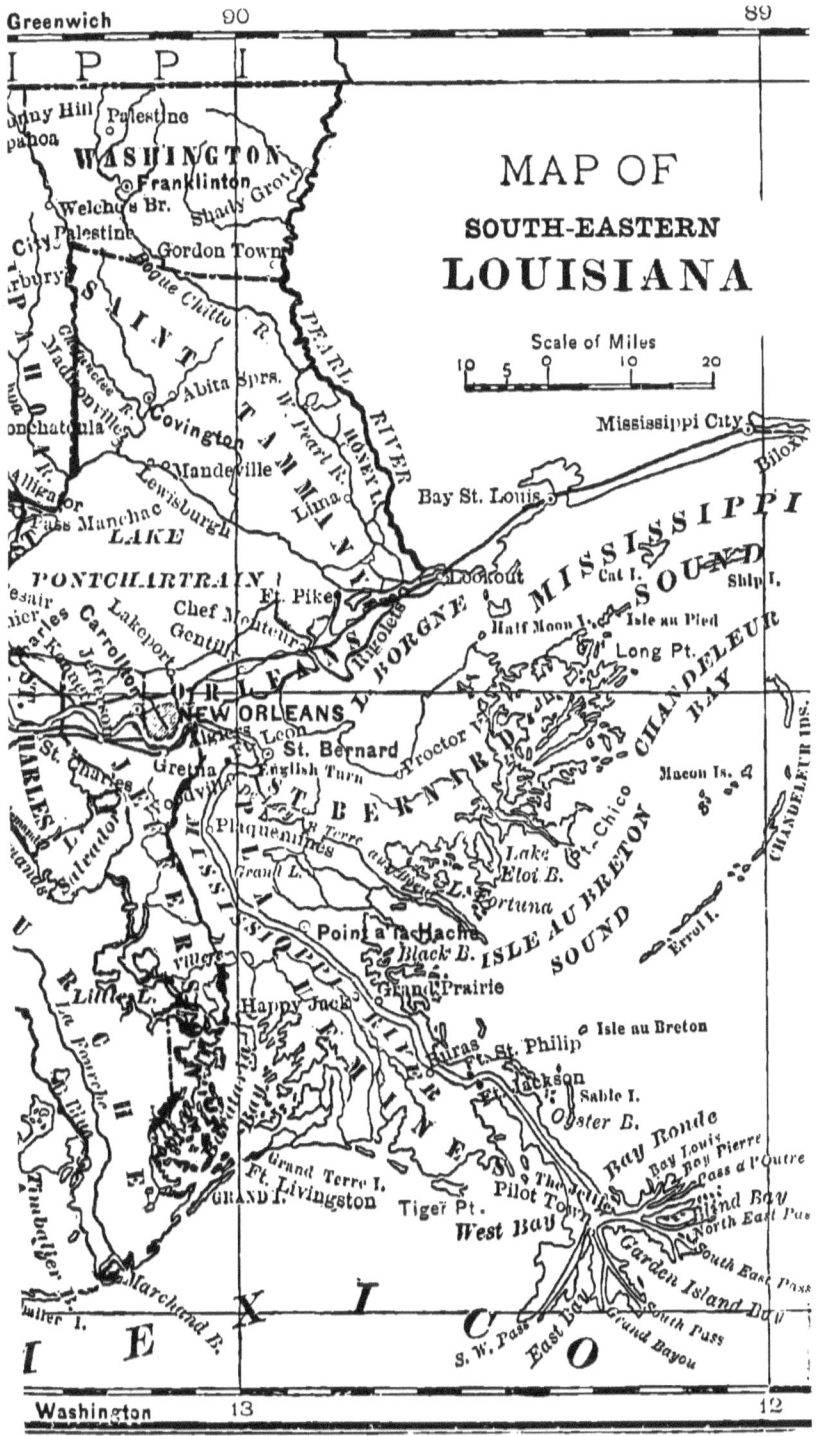

MAP OF

SOUTH-EASTERN

LOUISIANA

Scale of Miles

N. Y. Map & Relief Line Eng. Co. 17 Warren St.

How high is its highest point?

One hundred and eighty-five feet above the sea-level.

Which is the farthest to the east?

Belle Isle.

EACH OF THESE ISLANDS, with the exception of Belle Isle, is separated from its neighbor by a distance of about six miles. Belle Isle is distant from Cote Blanche, the most easterly of the four, about twenty-four miles.

For what is Petite Anse Island noted?

For its extensive mine of rock-salt.

THIS MINE is owned by Mr. Avery, who has established his salt works there. The salt is found between eleven and thirty feet below the surface of the earth. The miners have already worked down over sixty-five feet into the solid salt, which just shows itself on a level with tide water. It is supposed to extend hundreds of feet below the surface of the Gulf, and it has been found to be superior to any other salt found in the Southern market.

What do you notice in all the parishes bordering on the Gulf?

The great number of bayous, large and small, which cross them in every direction.

QUESTIONS ON THE MAP.

Which is the most southern of the Attakapas Parishes? What are the bays along the coast of St. Mary's Parish? What river, flowing into the Gulf of Mexico, forms part of the eastern boundary of St. Mary's? What lakes form another part of its eastern boundary? (P—e and G—d). In what Parish does Bayou Teche rise? Into what lake does Bayou Teche empty? Describe its course.

What large bayou rises in Red River, in Rapides Parish, and empties into Bayou Teche? State through what parishes it passes.

8

What parish is north-west of St. Mary's?   What bay opens partly into the coast of Iberia Parish and partly into that of Vermilion Parish?

What fresh water lakes are in Vermilion Parish?   What river flows from Grande Lake in that parish, into the Gulf? Of what two parishes does it form partly the boundary?   Bound Lafayette Parish?   St. Martin, Vermilion, Iberia, and St. Mary's.

Name the chief town in each.

CHAPTER VI.

THE GREAT PRAIRIE REGION.

"THE PRAIRIE is gently rolling, like the billows of a deep sea.   In fact, one cannot ride through the prairies without having their striking resemblance to large bodies of water constantly recurring to his mind.   The grass which grows upon their surface, waving in the wind, looks like ripples on the bosom of the ocean, the dark blue borders of woods are like distant shores, the projecting spurs like capes and promontories, the 'coves' like bays and gulfs, and the occasional clumps of detached trees like islands in the sea."—*Dennett's* "*Louisiana as it is.*"

How is the great Prairie Country bounded?
On the East by Bayou Têche ; on the North by Bayou Cocodric (in the northern part of St. Landry) ; on the South by the Sea-Marsh ; on the West by the Calcasieu and Sabine Rivers.

Name the parishes in which the prairies are mostly found?
St. Landry and a part of Calcasieu, Iberia, Cameron, Vermilion and St. Mary Parishes.

How was this region formerly known?
As the Opelousas and Attakapas Country.

How are the separate parishes formed?

Bayous, on which grow fine forests of trees, run through the entire prairie section. The belts of timber, jutting out into the open prairies, divide it into separate tracts, each with its own name.

Give the names of the principal of these tracts?

Faquetyke, Mamou, Calcasieu, Sabine, Vermilion, Mermentau, Plaquemines, Opelousas and Grande Prairie.

What may be said of the climate of the Prairie Region?

It is deliciously cool in the summer, and mild in the winter, and very healthy.

Where does it begin in St. Landry Parish?

Thirteen miles northwest of Opelousas, gradually opening to the southward.

What are to be seen at all times scattered over these prairies?

Vast herds of cattle and Creole ponies.

THESE ARE NOT REALLY WILD CATTLE. They belong to individuals, and when they reach a certain age, they are branded with the initials of the owners. But, in the sweep and grace of their movements, and in their timidity at the sight of man, they seem to be nearer to the wild herds that crowd Western prairies, than to the civilized droves of wealthy planters.

The Creole pony, although very small, is tough, wiry, and noted for great endurance. It is also famous as a racer.

What springs does St. Landry contain?

Some fine mineral springs, which are much visited by invalids.

QUESTIONS ON THE MAP.

Bound St. Landry. What is the chief town?

CHAPTER VII.

THE PINEY WOODS PARISHES.

Name the Piney Woods Parishes. Which of them are West of the Mississippi River? Which of them are East?

Why are they so called?

Because most of them are covered with great pine forests.

What is the character of the piney wood country?

It is quite open and has but little underbush.

With what is its surface covered?

With a coarse grass, which affords a fair pasturage in the spring.

What can you say of the soil?

It is, with few exceptions, poor and sandy.

Of the inhabitants?

They are plain and honest, virtuous and hospitable.

What spring is to be found in Calcasieu Parish?

A large mine of pure crystalline sulphur, near Lake Charles.

How was the mine first discovered?

Some parties, in boring for petroleum, accidentally struck the sulphur mine.

Has petroleum been found yet?

It is well known that petroleum does exist under the surface ; but it has not yet been discovered.

What is the principal industry in Calcasieu Parish?

The lumber business.

What has resulted from this business?

The establishment of numerous saw-mills, giving steady employment to a fleet of fifty or sixty schooners.

Where is this lumber carried?

To the ports of Texas and Mexico, and the West Indies.

It is estimated that, at least, four-fifths of the people of Calcasieu Parish depend, in one way or another, for a living, upon this timber business. The recent troubles in the parish, on account of the confiscation by the Government of logs cut on the public lands, cannot have been forgotten. The creed of the Calcasieu logmen may be summed up in these words : " *You take our logs, you take our bread from us.*"

By whom was the first settlement in Natchitoches Parish made?

By St. Denis, a relative of Bienville's.

Why had St. Denis gone to that country?

He had stopped there to see about establishing a trade with the Spanish colonies in Mexico.

By whom was the region inhabited at the time?

By the Natchitoches tribe of Indians.

Whom did he leave to make a settlement there?

A few Canadians, while he proceeded on his mission with the remainder of his men.

What State institution is near Alexandria?

The Louisiana University.

The State University was, a few years ago, destroyed by fire. After that, the University was removed to Baton Rouge. It will be continued there until the buildings can be rebuilt. It was lately united with the Agricultural and Mechanical College.

On what river is it situated?

On Red River.

Describe the course of Red River.

What watering places are in St. Tammany Parish?

Lewisburg and Mandeville.

Which is the largest Piney Wood Parish?
Calcasieu.

Which is the smallest?
Grant.

QUESTIONS ON THE MAP.

Into what river does Red River empty? In what parish is its mouth? Through what parishes does Red River first enter Louisiana, and from what State? Describe its course? What river forms the boundary between Catahoula and Concordia parishes? What between Catahoula and Grant? Into what lake does Little River flow and then issue? Describe its course? Into what river does Black River flow?

Which is the most northern of the Piney Woods Parishes west of the Mississippi? Which is the most eastern? Which is the most southern? Which the most western? What large lake is in Catahoula Parish? Which city in Rapides Parish is on Red River? Which in Natchitoches Parish is on the same river?

What large river flows into, and forms a part of Black River in Catahoula Parish? What river flows into the same river at or near the same point? What town is situated just between the two mouths? Describe the course of the Ouachita River? Which parishes does it first strike? Of what parishes does it form the boundary?

What large island is to be found in Catahoula Parish? How is that island formed? If by rivers what rivers? What river is called Black River near its mouth? Where is the source of that river? (It begins as a bayou, and springs from Lake Providence in Carroll Parish).

Bound Calcasieu Parish ; Catahoula, Grant, Natchitoches, Rapides, Vernon and Winn.

Name the chief towns in each?

EAST OF THE MISSISSIPPI.

Which is the most western of the Piney Woods Parishes east of the Mississippi? Which are the most eastern? Which

extends farthest south? What two border on Lake Pontchar-
train? Which of these two has the larger extent on that lake?
Which two border on Lake Maurepas? Which parish lies
directly North of New Orleans? On what lakes does St. Tam-
many Parish border? What is the eastern boundary of St.
Tammany and Washington parishes? From what State does
Pearl River flow?

How many branches has Pearl River near its mouth?
(Three—East Pearl, Middle Pearl and West Pearl, each having
its own mouth.) *In what parish do these branches unite into*
one stream? (In St. Tammany within about thirty miles from
the mouths.) *What river forms the boundary between East*
Baton Rouge and Livingston Parishes? What between St.
Helena and East Feliciana? Into what body of water does
that river flow?

Bound Livingston Parish, St. Helena, etc.
Name the chief town in each.

CHAPTER VIII.

THE GOOD UPLANDS PARISHES.

Name the Good Uplands Parishes.

Where do the good uplands mostly lie?
In North Louisiana.

Do they cover, or not, the entire surface of the parishes in
which they are found?
They cover only the larger part of those parishes.

Besides these parishes, what others also contain them?
Good uplands are to be found in the eastern part of
the two Felicianas, and in the north-eastern corner of
East Baton Rouge.

Why are those Parishes known as the Florida Parishes?

What is the general character of the good uplands region ?
It is extremely hilly.

What elevation do some of the ridges attain ?
The highest reach a height of at least three hundred feet above the valleys around them.

How high would this make them above the Gulf of Mexico?
Between four hundred and five hundred feet.

What peculiar lands are to be found in Sabine, Webster, Claiborne, Union, and Jackson Parishes?
Belts of land, several miles in length, known as " *Red lands.*"

Why is this name given to these lands?
Owing to a strong impregnation of iron, the soil is of a blood-red color.

What parishes have the best cotton land ?
De Soto, Bossier, Caddo, and Red River Parishes.

IT WAS IN DE SOTO PARISH that two of the great battles in Louisiana, during the Civil War were fought. The battle of Mansfield, April 8, 1864, and that of Pleasant Hill, April 9, 1864. These places are about eighteen miles distant. Mansfield is the court house town of the parish; and Pleasant Hill is in the south-eastern part near the Sabine Parish line.

What peculiarity do you notice about Caddo Parish?
The number of fresh-water lakes which, with the bayous running into one another, form almost as great a net-work of waters as in the Sea-Coast Parishes.

Give the names of some of these lakes.
Caddo Lake, Sodo Lake, Cross Lake and Clear Lake.

What curiosity is also found in Caddo Parish ?
The famous Red River Raft.

THE RED RIVER RAFT.

What is the Red River Raft?

It is a great raft of logs, big and small.

What has made that raft?

The immense mass of trunks of trees and drift-wood which have been brought down by the rapid current, and have become so fastened together that they cannot be moved.

Why do you call it immense?

It is said to be lodged and pressed together for a dis-
.tance above Shreveport of over seventy miles.

How is this terrible raft injurious?

It stops navigation, and sometimes causes great overflows in the Valley.

THIS CELEBRATED RAFT is one of the wonders of Louisiana. On the broad-rushing Mississippi, the logs may become lodged for a time; but they finally get separated and float down the stream, some to be gathered along the banks; some to find their way to the Gulf. But they never remain long enough together to form anything like a raft. The rafts that go down the Mississippi are altogether different; for upon them are men from the great west, who have bound the huge logs together, and, for their own use, steer their clumsy bark through the swift current.

THOSE WHO SEE RED RIVER in Louisiana, can form no idea of the wild and romantic scenery, in which its waters have taken their rise. They come from that famous, but barren table-land in northern Texas, known, far and wide, as EL LLANO ESTACADO (*El Leyano Es-tah cah-do*) or the "STAKED PLAIN." The Staked Plain is at a height of 2,450 feet above the sea-level.

For the first sixty miles, Red River rushes through steep banks, from five to six hundred feet in height, forming a gorge, from the top of which the river beneath, starting upon its long journey, that can end only when it is lost in the mighty Mississippi, hundreds and hundreds of feet below, appears a quiet stream enough.

After whom was Morehouse Parish named?

Mr. Morehouse was an American, to whom, in 1801, was ceded a grant by the Baron de Bastrop.

What Uplands Parishes were named after Indian tribes?

Caddo and Ouachita Parishes.

Tell the derivation of as many of the others as you can.

Of what origin are most of the inhabitants of North Louisiana?

Generally of English, Scotch or Irish descent, or immigrants from other States. They are an excellent class of people.

Can you describe a marked difference between South Louisiana and North Louisiana?

In South Louisiana, there are large plantations and few towns. In North Louisiana, there are a greater number of small farms and numerous thriving villages.

QUESTIONS ON THE MAP.

Which of the Good Uplands Parishes border on the Arkansas State Line? Which is the most eastern of these? Which the most western? Which extends the farthest south? Which contains the greatest extent of water surface? What long lake divides Bossier Parish from Bienville Parish? What river forms part of the boundary between De Soto Parish and Texas? Which are the first river parishes through which Red River enters into Louisiana? What lake extends from Caddo Parish into Texas? What other lakes are there in Caddo Parish? Bound Caddo Parish; De Soto; Sabine; Bossier; Webster; Red River; Claiborne; Bienville; Union; Jackson; Ouachita; Morehouse; Caldwell; East Feliciana and West Feliciana.

Name the chief towns in each.

What other important towns are there, and in what parish?

CHAPTER IX.

THE BLUFF LANDS.

What are known as the Bluff Lands?

High, steep lands found on the banks of the Mississippi and other rivers.

Can you mention any Bluff Land towns along the East bank of the Mississippi?

Baton Rouge, Port Hudson in Louisiana, Natchez and Vicksburg in Mississippi, and Memphis in Tennessee, are all Bluff cities.

Are there any on the West bank?

There are none immediately on the bank of the river, but some distance back.

Into what divisions are the Bluff Lands classed?

Into the hilly Bluff and the level Bluff.

Name a type of the hilly Bluff in Mississippi?

Vicksburg.

Name representatives of the level Bluff with deep ravines?

Port Hudson in Louisiana, and Natchez in Mississippi.

THE BLUFF LANDS begin, in the North, in Carroll Parish. They pass through Carroll, Richland and Franklin; are met with in Sicily Island, in Catahoula, Rapides, and Avoyelles Parishes; and going southward, are to be found in Washington, Opelousas and St. Landry, ending in those beautiful islands rising out of the gloomy sea marsh.

CHAPTER X.

LAKES.

Into what is the lake-system of Louisiana divided?
Iuto salt-water and fresh-water lakes.

In which class are the largest lakes found?
The former.

Can you give the extent of the lake surface of Louisiana?
Seventeen hundred square miles.

What does this include?
Both the salt-water and fresh-water lakes.

Which is the largest of the salt-water lakes?
Lake Pontchartrain.

In honor of whom was Lake Pontchartrain named?
Which is the next salt lake in size?
Who can tell why it received its present name?

What do the shores of these larger salt-water lakes afford?
Most healthy and attractive homes during the summer months.

THE PRINCIPAL WATERING PLACES, such as Shieldsboro' (Bay St. Louis,) Pass Christian, Biloxi and Pascagoula, are along what is known as the Mississippi Sound, in the State of Mississippi. But it is well known that those on the North shore of Lake Pontchartrain, in St. Tammany Parish, cannot be surpassed for pure air and pleasant residences. Lewisburg and Mandeville are favorite watering places on that coast.

What is to be noted in St. Bernard Parish?
The great number of small salt-water lakes, which are to be found scattered throughout its surface.

With what body of water do these lakes connect?
The Gulf of Mexico.

In what parishes are to be found the largest fresh-water lakes?

In St. Charles, Assumption, Iberia, Vermilion, Cameron, Catahoula, Bienville, Bossier and Caddo Parishes.

Give the names of the principal of these lakes, and the Parishes in which they are?

Lake des Allemands and Washa Lake .... St. Charles
Verret Lake.................... .... Assumption
White Lake and Grand Lake .... Vermilion
Calcasieu Lake............................. Cameron
Catahoula Lake............................. Catahoula
Lake Bistineau....... .... Bienville
Lake Bodeau.... .... Bossier
Saline Lake................................. Winn
Caddo Lake ⎫
Sodo Lake ⎬ .... Caddo
Cross Lake ⎭

Which large fresh water lake forms the boundary between Jefferson and St. Charles Parishes?

Lake Salvador, or Lake Washa, as it is more generally known.

Which washes portions of Iberia, St. Martin's, St. Mary, and Assumption Parishes?

Grand Lake.

QUESTIONS ON THE MAP.

SALT WATER LAKES.

What is the most eastern great salt water lake near New Orleans? Which is the most western? Which is the centre lake? Is it larger or smaller than the others? If larger, is it larger than both of them together? What parishes border on Lake Pontchartrain? Which on Lake Maurepas? Which on Lake Borgne? What strait connects Lakes Pontchartrain and Borgne? What pass connects them farther west? Into what sound does Lake Borgne open? What lake, with a bay of the same name, is in Terrebonne Parish? What lake is at the south-western extremity of Louisiana? What large river empties into Sabine Lake? How is Sabine Lake connected with the Gulf of Mexico?

FRESH WATER LAKES.

Which is the farthest north? What lake in Caddo Parish is partly in Texas? What lake forms the boundary between Bienville and Bossier Parishes?

What large lake in Cameron Parish reaches the boundary of Calcasieu? Through what pass does that lake reach the Gulf? What lake in Catahoula Parish? What lake in Bossier? With what river does it connect by bayous on the west? What bayou flows into it from a northerly direction?

CHAPTER XI.

BAYS.

What parishes contain the greatest number of small bays?
Plaquemines and Jefferson Parishes.

What do these numerous bays form?
A large portion of the southern part of these two parishes.

What famous bay lies between them?
Barataria Bay.

For what is this bay noted?
For the superior oysters which are found in it, and in the bayous flowing into it.

LOVERS OF GOOD OYSTERS outside of Louisiana, acknowledge that there are no finer oysters in the country than those of Barataria Bay and vicinity. Louisianians boast that the Baratarian oysters have no equal anywhere.

What bays indent the stretch of land forming the mouth of the Mississippi?

Blind Bay, Garden Island Bay and East Bay.

THE MOUTH OF THE MISSISSIPPI may be likened in appearance to the leg and claw of a chicken. The long narrow strip from Fort Jackson and Fort Philip is the leg ; and the different Passes make up a strong resemblance to the claw.

.

QUESTIONS ON THE MAP.

What part of the Gulf coast of Louisiana contains all the bays ? In what parish does this section of bays begin from the east ? In what parish does it end ? Which is the most easterly bay ? The most southerly ? The most westerly ? Which extends farthest to the north ? Which next ? Off what parishes are these last bays ? What bays are west of Vermilion ?

What four bays indent Terrebonne Parish ? Which parish contains more bays than any other ? How many are there ? Name them ? Where is Caillou Bay ? What four bays are south of the Parishes of St. Mary, Iberia, and Vermilion Parishes ? Which of these parishes has the greatest bay extent ? Which the smallest ?

By what pass are the waters of Barataria Bay and the Gulf connected ? Which do you think the most open bay along the coast ? (C—u Bay.) Which do you think the most closed ? (F—r L—e B.)

What pass connects the waters of Timbalier Bay with the Gulf ? What lake unites Caillou and Terrebonne Bays ? (Lake Pelto.)

LAKE PELTO is not really a lake, as it is not entirely surrounded by land. It is properly a strait connecting Caillou and Terrebonne Bays. There are some very fine oyster-beds in this lake, near Last Island.

Which is farther east, Terrebonne or Timbalier Bay ? Is Caillou Bay to the east or west of them ?

CHAPTER XII.

ISLANDS.

How may the islands in Louisiana be divided?

Into outlying islands and sea-marsh islands.

What are the outlying islands?

Those which lie outside of the coast line in the Gulf of Mexico.

What are the sea-marsh islands?

Name some of the best known outlying islands.

Chandeleur, Errol, Grand Isle, Timbalier, and Last Island.

For what is Grand Isle noted?

For its splendid surf bathing.

What sad story is connected with Last Island?

In August, 1856, one hundred lives were lost in a terrible storm which submerged the island.

BEFORE THAT TIME, Last Island had been a favorite watering place.

What island lies in front of Barataria Bay?

Grande Terre Island.

Who can tell what made this island famous in history? (See History, Chapter XXXVI.)

GRAND ISLAND and the islands around it are said to be still inhabited by the descendants of Lafitte's men.

This entire section was the headquarters of Lafitte and his companions. About here, they anchored their fleet when they had come from a long cruise. Here, they burned the prizes which they had captured. Here, they had many a wild frolic after a dangerous journey; and here, when they grew tired of their wild life, they settled down and became peaceful fishermen and hunters.

MISSISSIPPI JETTIES.

Can you name a large island in the interior ?

Sicily Island.

In what parish is Sicily Island?

QUESTIONS ON THE MAP.

Which are the most easterly islands ? What bay separates Chandeleur Island from the coast ? Of what Parish is that coast ? What sound is between Errol Island and the coast ? Which is farther east, Grande Terre Island or Grand Island ? Off what parish are they ? What island lies stretched across Timbalier Bay ? What two lie in front of Terrebonne Bay ? What long island lies south of Terrebonne Parish ? What lake divides it from the parish ? What large islana lies between Vermilion Bay and the Bay of St. Bernard ? What, from its name, would you judge that island to be ? In what parish is Sicily Island ? How is it formed ? In what parish is Honey Island ? How formed ?

CHAPTER XIII.

THE MISSISSIPPI RIVER AND THE JETTIES.

Taking all its bends together, the Mississippi has a length of eight hundred miles through Louisiana. Its great tributary in the State is the Red River. Besides the Red River, it receives, in its progress from its source to its mouth, the waters of many large tributaries.

What is a source of pride to Louisianians?

That it is through their State that the "Father of Waters," the mighty Mississippi, rushes to the Gulf.

What can you say of this great river ?

That it pours a larger body of water, through more thousands of miles of country, filled with cities, towns, villages and farms, than any other river.

In what does its great rival, the Amazon, differ from it ?

In this, that more than three-fourths of the course

of that river lies through pathless wilds and savage tribes.

In CERTAIN SEASONS OF THE YEAR, that is, during the late winter and the early spring, the Mississippi overflows the low banks which lie along its course, on both sides from Baton Rouge to its mouth. Baton Rouge is situated on the first high banks, or bluffs, which are to be seen in ascending the river.

As a protection against these annual overflows, banks of earth called LEVEES, have been built all along both sides of the river.

Sometimes, it happens that the high waters break through these banks. This is what is called a *Crévasse*—a French word which means a breaking or piercing through—and which often destroys a vast amount of property before it can be stopped. In the spring of 1874, thirty-one parishes were overflowed.

THE JETTIES.

Is the Lower Mississippi much troubled from want of water?

Never much, save at its mouth.

What is the matter at the mouth?

The immense amount of mud and sand, carried down by the current for thousands of miles, meeting the waters of the Gulf, is brought to a sudden check, and settles in the different Passes at the mouth.

How many passes are there ?   What do they resemble ?

In what does this result?

The water has, through long years, become too shallow for the passage of large ships.

Have efforts ever been made to deepen the water at the mouth?

Often ; and millions of dollars have been spent upon experiments.

With what success?

Not much, until lately.   All but one of the Passes became closed.

Can you name the Pass that remained open?
The South-west Pass.

Is the South-west Pass still open?
Yes, it is still used by the largest vessels ; but scientific men say that the water in that Pass is getting shallower and shallower every day.

Has any attempt been made to open one of the other Passes?
There has been one made to open the South Pass.

Who has taken charge of this work?
Captain JAMES B. EADS.

What work has Capt. Eads constructed?
One that he calls the "JETTIES."

Describe the Jetties.
THE JETTIES consist of two parallel rows of piling, driven into the mud twelve feet apart. These rows are planked strongly on the inside. Then they are filled with small willow trees, lashed together, and generally called " mattrasses,"—and with stones and rocks and earth.

What do these two rows make?
Two artificial banks.

How far are the banks apart?
One thousand feet.

How far do they extend?
Two and a half (2½) miles, from deep water in the river, to deep water in the Gulf.

How can you describe the effect of these banks?
They keep the mud and the sand from being scattered about in the water, and bring them within a narrow space for the swift current to play upon them, and to wash them away into the Gulf.

THE MASS OF MUD AND SAND between these strong banks is about nine hundred feet wide. With the fierce current of the Mississippi—the Giant, as it is the Father, of Rivers—playing upon it, stirring it round and round, and washing it out, it is believed that it will be swept out of the Pass as fast as it is brought into it.

Already vessels, drawing twenty-one feet, have passed successfully through the SOUTH PASS. The best judges have no doubt of the final success of Captain Eads' Jetties.

CHAPTER XIV.

BAYOUS.

What is one of the most marked features of Louisiana scenery?

The great number of bayous to be found within its limits.

What is this name of " bayou " ?

A *French* word given by the earliest French settlers.

UN BOYAU, a gut, an intestine. Corrupted by the early and ignorant settlers of the colony of Louisiana into *bayou.* The word gut, as a leader, a vehicle, a conductor, is found in most perfected languages. We find it especially in the *gut*, or bayou of Skeggereck, or Kategut.

OWING TO THE ALMOST INEXTRICABLE NET-WORK of streams, scattered throughout the State, it is not strange that this word has been given a special meaning. There is no water-course in any State—except, perhaps, Florida—precisely like the Louisiana bayous. Settlers from other States never saw, in their old homes, anything nearer to them than their creeks; and " creeks " are not " bayous."

Along the banks of bayous—which are not very far apart, either, as a rule—the trees seem, somehow, to be thicker, and their branches to lean more lovingly over the water flowing beneath them. Sometimes, these branches meet in a thick arch, through the leaves of which the sun, even at mid-day, cannot shine. Everything is strange here—everything is mysterious, at the broadest noon. And, when the darkness of night comes on, and there are belated travelers passing on through the blackness from one bayou into another, the scene seems to become, at once, solemn as well as mysterious. The same scenes and sounds are there; the same great trees rise close to the banks; the same ghostly moss hangs, high and low, in the air, from the big branches; the same cranes—now mostly asleep—are still standing, who can tell? one leg in the water; and the same roar of the sleepless alligator is heard thundering from every side—but all of these appear, in some way, to have changed. Night has fallen upon the bayous.

What can you say about the depth of the bayous?
It is not the same at different times of the year.

How is that?
They are shallow during the dry season; but when the rains fall, and in the early spring, they often overflow their banks.

What precaution has been taken against such overflows?
The building of levees along the banks.

A LEVEE IS AN ARTIFICIAL BANK OF EARTH—that is, a bank raised by men on the low grounds lying along rivers and bayous, to protect their waters from overflowing them. These levees, of course, are always much higher than the ground itself. Sometimes, the waters happen to break through them. Then, there is what is called a *crevasse.* And, before the hole made by this *crevasse* is filled up, an immense loss of property and stock, and ruined fields and crops, is the result.

Is the current of bayous strong or slow?
It is both.

What do you mean by that?
It is slow or sluggish when the bayou is low.

Suppose that the bayou is high?
It, then, generally runs strongly in the direction of the stream in which it happens to flow.

Are all the bayous navigable to steamboats in the high-water season ?

Very few of them are.

Name some of them that are navigable.

The LAFOURCHE, COURTABLEAU, CYPREMORT, and TECHE Bayous.

You have said, have you not, that a bayou must flow from some other stream ?

Yes ; it is never fed by springs.

Of what character may such streams be ?

They may flow from a river, or a lake, or from another bayou.

Can you mention two bayous flowing from a river ?

Bayou PLAQUEMINES and Bayou LAFOURCHE.

THE PLAQUEMINES leaves the Mississippi about twenty-two miles below Baton Rouge. The LAFOURCHE leaves the same river about thirty miles before that point.

Who of the class can give an idea of the course of these bayous ? Into what streams do they flow?

What peculiarity may be noticed about Bayou Lafourche ?

It receives no tributary streams.

What do you mean by that ?

I mean that no other stream flows *into* it.

Does that mean that there are no streams flowing from it ?

Not at all ; because bayous flow from it all its length.

Well then, what is your idea of really " tributary streams ? "

Those that add water to a stream, in other words, pay tribute to it.

IN THE OLD DAYS of the world, " tribute " was a sum, large or small, paid by an inferior to his superior lord. As every stream that runs *into* another stream adds water to that stream, it is the custom to call it a "tributary." In other words, the stream that runs into another renders *tribute* to it.

Can you mention a bayou formed by the junction of two bayous?

Bayou COURTABLEAU.

By the junction of what two bayous is Bayou Courtableau formed?

By that of Bayous COCODRIE and BŒUF.

THIS NAME OF COCODRIE is supposed to be a corruption of the French word *crocodile*, the same as our English word " crocodile."

Can you give the name of a bayou flowing from a lake?

What do you observe in regard to some bayous?

Some of them are long and deep, and broad enough to be often called " rivers."

Name some of those streams called either "bayous" or "rivers."

The ATCHAFALAYA, LAFOURCHE, BŒUF, and MAÇON.

Describe the course of the Atchafalaya.
Describe that of the Bœuf.
Describe that of the Maçon.

You have mentioned Bayou Bœuf: what peculiarity do you observe about this name?

Several streams in the State bear the same name.

Can you tell how many bayous of the same name there are?

There are at least three Bayous BŒUF.

Which is the most southern of these?

That which is formed from several streams that rise east of Lake Palourde.

Is this Bayou Bœuf as important as the others?

It is not; it is scarcely important enough to be put on the map.

Where is the second Bayou Bœuf?

It begins in Rapides Parish, runs through a part of St. Landry, and, while still in that parish, with the aid of Bayou COCODRIE, forms Bayou COURTABLEAU.

Where is the third Bayou Bœuf?

In the Northern part of the State.

Describe its course.

After crossing the Arkansas Line, it finally flows into the Ouachita River.

THIS BAYOU BŒUF is really a river, and it is generally so called. From its source in the Arkansas Lakes to its junction with the Ouachita, its length is nearly two hundred and forty miles.

You have said that several streams bear this same name of Bayou Bœuf, although one of them, at least, is a river; what does the difference existing between them show?

The very vague idea that the early settlers had of what was really a bayou.

THE MAÇON is another instance of a stream—really a river— often classed as a bayou. The Maçon issues from the large lakes in Arkansas, and receives, in its course towards the South, many other outlets—particularly, the Tensas. After the junction of these two streams, east of Sicily Island, they take the name of the Tensas River.

Who can tell in what parts of Louisiana the bayous seem to be most numerous?

As a rule, in South-western and North-western Louisiana.

What, after thinking a little about the matter, would you call the deepest and broadest bayous?

Those flowing into the Gulf of Mexico, or the lakes near the Gulf.

You have seen how close a net-work the bayous make in some parts of your State ; now, what do you think are the uses of bayous?

First, their waters give fish for all living upon their banks.

What other use have they?

They enable the inhabitants to pass easily from one point to another, and to convey their merchandise upon their waters.

These are two uses : Who can tell the third?

The lands along the bayous are generally alluvial.

And, if "alluvial," what must those lands be?

Among the most fertile and the richest in the State.

THIS CHAPTER has not tried to give more than an idea of the remarkable system of waters (known as BAYOUS) to be found in the State of Louisiana. Their real character—their real number —their real importance, contain enough points of interest to make up a large volume. AUDUBON has written eloquently of the "birds of Louisiana." Some day, a man—as great in his work as AUDUBON was in his—will tell the story of the bayous of Louisiana.

9

POPULATION OF LARGE CITIES, TOWNS AND VILLAGES IN LOUISIANA.

(CENSUS OF 1870.)

Name of City, Town or Village.	Where situated.	Population.
New Orleans	Mississippi River	191418
Baton Rouge	" "	6498
Shreveport	Red River	4650
Monroe	Ouachita River	1949
Thibodaux	Bayou Lafourche	1922
Donaldsonville	Mississippi River	1573
Opelousas	Bayou Bellevue	1546
Plaquemines	Mississippi River	1460
Natchitoches	Cane River	1401
New Iberia	Bayou Têche	1400
Franklin	" "	1265
Alexandria	Red River	1218
St. Martinsville	Bayou Têche	1190
Morgan City	Morgan R. R.	1000
Clinton	Inland	1000
Jackson	"	934
Vermilionville	Near Vermilion River	925
Amite City	Jackson R. R.	910
Washington	Bayou Bœuf	907
Bastrop	Inland	900
Gretna	Opposite New Orleans	900
Houma	Bayou Terrebonne	875
Lake Providence	Mississippi River	850
Mansfield	Inland	813
Lake Charles	Lake Charles	800
Bonnet Carré	Mississippi River	725
Bayou Sara	" "	675
Trenton	Ouachita River	600
Farmerville	Inland	600
Covington	Near the Chefunctee	585
Convent	Mississippi River	550
Abbeville	Vermilion River	545
Homer	Inland	525
Pineville	Red River	525
Waterproof	Mississippi River	525
Delta	" "	500
Minden	Inland	500

TABLE OF PARISHES WITH THEIR POPU- LATIONS (ACCORDING TO THE CENSUS OF 1870).

Ascension	11,577	Natchitoches	18,265
Assumption	13,234	Orleans	191,418
Avoyelles	12,926	Ouachita	11,582
Bienville	10,636	Plaquemines	10,552
Bossier	12,675	Point Coupée	12,981
Caddo	21,714	Rapides	18,015
Calcasieu	6,733	Richland	5,110
Caldwell	4,820	Sabine	6,496
Cameron	1,591	St. Bernard	3,553
Carroll	10,110	St. Charles	4,867
Catahoula	8,475	St. Helena	5,423
Claiborne	20,240	St. James	10,152
Concordia	9,977	St. John Baptist	6,762
De Soto	14,962	St. Landry	25,553
East Baton Rouge	17,816	St. Martin	9,370
East Feliciana	13,499	St. Mary	13,860
Franklin	5,078	St. Tammany	5,586
Grant	4,517	Tangipahoa	7,928
Iberia	9,042	Tensas	12,419
Iberville	12,347	Terrebonne	12,451
Jackson	7,646	Union	11,685
Jefferson	17,767	Vermilion	4,528
Lafayette	10,388	Washington	3,830
Lafourche	14,719	West Baton Rouge	5,114
Livingston	4,026	West Feliciana	10,499
Madison	8,600	Winn	4,954
Morehouse	9,387		

Total of Population of State............ 726,915

TABLE OF PRINCIPAL ISLANDS, LAKES, RIVERS AND BAYOUS IN LOUISIANA.

ISLANDS.

Au Breton.	East Timbalier.	Sable.
Au Pied.	Grand.	Shell.
Batledor.	Grande Terre.	St. Johns.
Bird.	Maçons.	Timbalier.
Caillou.	Marsh.	Vidal.
Chandeleur.	Profit.	Vine.
Coopers.	Rabbit.	

LAKES.

Arthur.	Fields.	Peigneur.
Bayou Pierre.	Grand (2).	Pontchartrain.
Bistineau.	Grass.	Quitman's.
Black Lake (2)·	Jatt.	Round.
Bodeau.	Léry.	Sabine.
Borgne.	Little.	Saline.
Caddo.	Long.	Sancosan.
Caillou.	Maurepas	Sodo.
Calcasieu.	Méchant.	Spanish.
Canhisnia (2).	Mill.	Swan.
Catahoula.	Moreau.	Tasse.
Charles.	Mud (2).	Verret.
Chicot.	Natchez (2).	Wallace's.
Cross.	Oskibe.	Washa (or Salvador.)
De Corde.	Palourde.	White.
Des Allemands.	Pearl.	

RIVERS.

Amite.	Dugdemona.	Red.
Atchafalaya.	Little.	Sabine.
Black.	Maçon.	Tangipahoa.
Bœuf.	Mermenton.	Tensas.
Calcasieu.	Mississippi.	Tickfaw.
Cane.	Ouachita.	Vermilion.
Chefunctee.	Pearl.	

BAYOUS.

Black Bayou.	De Large.	Nezpiquè.
Black Lake Bayou.	Des Allemands.	Plaquemine.
Blue Bayou.	Grand Caillou.	Petit Caillou.
Bodeau.	Grossetête.	Phalia.
Bœuf.	Lacassane.	Queue de Tortue.
Courtableau.	Lafourche.	Saline.
Dorchite.	Lanacoco.	Têche.
De Glaize.	Maçon.	Terrebonne.

PART III.

PRODUCTS.

CHAPTER I.

What are the products of a State?

Whatever that State produces.

What is understood by this definition?

All that is produced upon its soil, or below its surface.

UNDER THIS HEAD OF PRODUCTS (although not strictly belonging to them) are generally included all the varieties of its animals, wild or tame—the birds in its woods, and the fishes in its waters.

Name some of the products of Louisiana produced upon the soil.

Sugar-cane, cotton, rice, indigo, tobacco, hay, wheat, rye, fruits, and vegetables.

What do you also include in this class?

The splendid growth of forest trees for which Louisiana is famous.

Name what you consider as produced below the surface.

Minerals, such as salt, sulphur, gypsum, etc.

What can be said of the productive capacity of the soil of Louisiana?

It is acknowledged to be greater than that of any other State in the Union.

What renders it so?

The wonderful fertility of its alluvial lands—the richest in the world.

What are known as alluvial lands?

What used to be the most valuable product, when Louisiana was a French and Spanish colony?

Indigo.

When did its value begin to diminish?

When it was seen that the cultivation of sugar-cane would be more profitable than that of indigo.

INDIGO is now cultivated to a limited extent only, and principally in the Attakapas Parishes.

CHAPTER II.

SUGAR.

In what year was the sugar-cane first introduced into Louisiana?

From what place was it brought? By whom?

Was it successfully cultivated at that time? If not, why?

When and by whom was it successfully cultivated finally?

What is the sugar-cane regarded?

As the most valuable product of Louisiana.

How do Louisiana sugar and molasses stand in the markets of the world?

They are unmistakably admitted to be superior to any other.

Are all the sugar-lands in Louisiana fit for the cultivation of the sugar-cane?

Only a very small part of them are.

To what is this owing?

To the want of hands to work all the cane-growing lands.

What would Louisiana, if properly cultivated, be capable of producing?

All the sugar-cane and molasses needed in the United States.

As A PROOF of how small is the amount of Louisiana sugar actually used in the country, it was estimated that, for the year 1874, the United States consumed :

Domestic Sugars .... 48,500 tons
Foreign " .. .. 661,869 "
Domestic Molasses.... .... 8,699,990 gals.
Foreign " .... 3,950,627 "

Where is the best sugar-cane raised?
In the Alluvial Parishes, although it also grows well in the Sea-Marsh Parishes.

Which is the great sugar-raising parish?
St. Mary's.

What others follow St. Mary in order in the crop of 1876?
Assumption, Ascension, St. James, Iberville, Terrebonne, Lafourche, Plaquemines, and St. John the Baptist.

CHAPTER III.

COTTON.

In what parishes are the best cotton lands found?
De Soto, Caddo, and Red River Parishes.

Along what river are most of these lands?
Red River.

Where is the cotton belt of the Southern States?
About thirty-two degrees North.

What is understood by the term "true cotton belt"?
A line below which cotton cannot be successfully cultivated, but above which it cannot be grown.

THE TECHE COUNTRY, however, is an exception to this. Although below the cotton belt, its fertile soil produces superior cotton. But there is nothing to wonder at in this; for is not the Têche country the "Garden of Louisiana?"

What species of cotton can be cultivated below it?
The species known as Sea Island cotton.

THE GREAT STATE for the cultivation of Sea Island cotton is South Carolina. It is one of the most valuable products of that State. In Louisiana the production is limited.

Where does the Sea Island cotton grow?
In the various Sea-Marsh Islands near the Gulf of Mexico.

How is cotton planted?
In rows extending the whole length of the field.

What is the usual distance between these rows?
Between two and a half to three feet.

Does the cotton plant grow to the same height everywhere?
No, it varies, according to the soil, from four to six, and, even seven, feet.

THE COTTON IS GENERALLY READY FOR PICKING in July. It is taken to the gin-house where it is ginned and then pressed into bales, then sent to the cities, where it is again pressed and made into still smaller bales. The average price for a bale of cotton is fifty dollars. Like that of sugar, the cultivation of cotton has much diminished since the war. In 1860, the cotton crop numbered 777,738 bales. In 1876, it reached nearly 300,000. It is increasing, however, every year.

What new industry has recently been started in New Orleans?
The manufacture of cotton seed oil.

From what is the oil manufactured?
From the cotton seed after the cotton is picked from it. This was formerly thrown away as useless

What is the process?
The oily cotton seeds are submitted to a strong pres-

sure by powerful machinery, until a valuable and pleasant smelling and tasting oil is obtained.

For what is this oil useful?

In a purified state, it is employed for what all other kinds of oils and fats are useful.

THE PRODUCTION of this oil has been advancing steadily. Large quantities are annually exported from New Orleans to Europe.

CHAPTER IV.

RICE.

What culture has rapidly increased within late years?

That of rice.

Where is rice principally produced?

In the alluvial and Attakapas Parishes.

THE FOLLOWING PARISHES produced the largest quantity of Rice for the year 1874-5 : Plaquemines, Lafourche, and St. Charles. Total crop of the State, 104,415 barrels.

What does rice most need for a healthy growth?

Plenty of water and a proper system of drainage.

Where does rice grow best?

In low and wet lands—lands too low and wet for corn, cotton, or sugar-cane.

When is it planted?

The planting season extends through March and April into May.

How long does the crop take to mature?

In four months or less. The harvest is generally in August.

Describe how the rice is cultivated?

When the rice has sprouted, the field is flooded, and the water is allowed to cover it several weeks. Then it is drained off. It is flooded a second time; and when it is drained off again, the rice is ready for reaping.

What will an acre produce in rice?

Seven barrels are a good average for a flooded crop.

How many pounds does a barrel hold?

A barrel contains two hundred and thirty pounds of clean rice.

THE RICE as it is taken from the field is called "*rough rice.*" It is taken to the mill where it is cleaned for one cent a pound. Rough rice weighs only one hundred and sixty-two pounds to the barrel. There are nearly twenty rice-mills in the State—most of them being situated in Plaquemines Parish, which is a very productive rice parish.

CHAPTER V.

FRUITS.

What can be said of Louisiana as a fruit growing State?

That she can grow almost every fruit that is to be found in more northern States.

What else may be said of her?

That many fruits which belong only to the tropics grow well on her soil.

Into what kinds are they divided?

Into cultivated fruits and wild fruits.

Name some of the former.

Japan plums, figs, oranges, cherries, peaches, grapes, pears, olives, dates, almonds, pine-apples, citrons, bananas, lemons, limes, shaddocks, strawberries, and the Chinese quince.

Name some of the latter.

Dewberries, blackberries, mulberries, chinquapins, wild strawberries, and the excellent muscadine grape, or black scuppernong.

What beautiful evergreen, as large as the orange, blossoms in the fall?

The Mespilus, or Japan plum tree.

THIS is a fine plum, yellow, and of a pleasant acid taste.

What is the best soil for grapes?

The soil of the pine-lands.

What section of Louisiana is best adapted to fruit growing?

The Coast Parishes.

ORANGES.

What is the most valuable fruit of Louisiana?

The orange.

What term has been given to the orange?

The "Queen of Fruits."

What varieties are there of oranges in Louisiana?

Nine, the principal of which are the sweet, sour, myrtle, mandarin and Brazilian.

THE ORANGE TREE is an evergreen. There is nothing prettier in the woods in mid-winter than its leaves of rich deep green. The spring brings no purer flowers in her train than its white blossoms, nor the autumn any richer ornament than its golden fruitage.

Which are the best orange parishes?

St. Bernard, Plaquemines, Orleans, Jefferson, St. Charles, St. John Baptist, St. James, Assumption,

Lafourche, Terrebonne, St. Mary, Iberia, Vermilion, Cameron and Sabine.

When do trees generally begin bearing?
When they are six or seven years old.

When are they considered to be full grown?
When they are about twelve or fifteen years old. They are productive to a good old age.

What is the usual yield of a full grown healthy tree?
From three to five thousand oranges.

A FLOUR BARREL WILL HOLD from three to four hundred oranges. On the trees, oranges generally sell at ten dollars a thousand. The largest orchards produce over three million oranges yearly, at a market value, therefore, of thirty thousand dollars to the owner. The average orange crop of the State amounts to about seventy thousand barrels.

How many orange trees are planted to one acre?
From one hundred to one hundred and twenty-five trees are planted.

How far are they planted apart?
From fifteen to twenty feet apart.

How many acres of orange trees are there in the State?
Probably fifteen hundred acres.

THE DEMAND throughout the country for Louisiana oranges is greater than the supply. Her best oranges are considered sweeter and more luscious than those that come from Cuba.

FIGS.

What native fruit of Louisiana should rank next in value to the orange?
The Fig.

Why is it of less value than the orange?
Because, like many of the tropical fruits, they soon turn acid, and cannot stand transportation.

How many varieties are cultivated in Louisiana ?
Twolve or fifteen.

Which variety is considered the best ?
The celeste or sugar fig.

How many crops does the fig tree bear ?
Three, the second only is valuable.

How long does the fig tree bear fruit ?
For fifty years, and sometimes more.

THE FIG is one of the most prolific of fruits and in dry, settled weather attains its greatest perfection.

Every morning, during the season, this fruit, cool from the night dews, can be gathered fresh for the breakfast table.

GRAPES.

What can you say of the native grapes of Louisiana ?
Many of them are highly prized. The Red River grape of this State has been introduced into France.

What lands are specially adapted to grape culture ?
The pine lands.

What two varieties are more extensively cultivated in Louisiana than others?
The Scuppernong and the Muscadine.

THE SCUPPERNONG is cultivated from the Gulf to the Ohio River, and succeeds in almost any soil. With proper care, a single vine will produce enough fruit, and furnish enough wine, for a family.

BANANAS.

How do bananas flourish in Louisiana?
They do well in the latitude of New Orleans and, when the winter is mild, as high up as thirty degrees.

At what season do they ripen ?
In the month of October.

CHAPTER VI.

FORESTS.

What do you know of the Louisiana forests?

They are always magnificent, and include many varieties of stately trees and beautiful vines.

Where is the principal forest growth to be found?

From the open prairie near the Têche, to the Atchafalaya, the eastern limits of St. Martin.

What valuable timber is to be found in the Atchafalaya swamps?

Millions of cypress trees, tall and straight. Many of them are from three to four feet in diameter.

How is this forest wealth made available?

It is cut and floated out, by means of rafts, for the use of saw-mills along the Mississippi River. .

Are there many other important trees to be found in our forests?

Yes, nearly all that are valuable for commercial purposes, and many others which give the charm of romance to our scenery.

Mention some that are articles of commerce.

Stout oaks, of numerous varieties, lofty pines, graceful willows, rapid-growing chinas, stately beeches, valuable ashes, enduring catalpas, and many others.

Which are the trees that have so often figured in romance and poetry?

The stately magnolia with its large, creamy blossoms, the fan-like palmetto, beautiful elms, gloomy cedars and the shadowy, moss-hung cypress.

What tree is most valuable in the Louisiana kitchen?

The sassafras tree, from the leaves of which the Creoles make their celebrated " gombo " powder.

What is a marked feature of Louisiana forests?

The drifting, clinging, funereal Spanish moss,—which embraces a tree only to kill it.

Where is this moss principally found?

All over South-western Louisiana, in the cypress swamps or along their borders.

How does this moss affect the landscape?

It shuts out all brightness, and gives a gloomy, weird-like aspect to the scene, even at noon.

Does this moss ever grow upon a dead tree?

No, when the tree dies the moss turns black, as though mourning for its mother, and drops off.

How does the moss benefit the swamp?

By absorbing the poisonous elements, it purifies the surrounding air.

THE SPANISH MOSS is an article of great commercial importance to Louisiana. The best moss comes from the Atchafalaya basin. There, the woodmen, in canoes, push their way through the bayous, gloomy even at mid-day, and gather it from the trees by means of long poles armed with hooks. It is then cured and dried, packed in bales and sent to the city factories, where it is prepared for final shipment.

Moss is sent from New Orleans to all parts of the United States, and even across the ocean to Europe.

What peculiarity of waters is to be observed in connection with the forests of Louisiana?

They are crossed in every direction by navigable bayous.

What purpose do these bayous serve?

They serve as natural drains for the land, and add to the picturesque beauty of the forests.

CHAPTER VII.

MINOR INDUSTRIES.

SILK WORMS.

What minor industry is practised in Louisiana?
The culture of silk worms.

What are silk worms?
Small caterpillars, that spin a curious covering of silk.

What are these coverings called?
Cocoons.

What becomes of the caterpillars?
They are killed after reaching a certain age, in order to rob them of their silk.

Why are they not allowed to live?
Because, in trying to get out of the cocoon, they cut it into little bits and so spoil the silk.

What do the worms live on?
Mulberry leaves.

Is the raising of silk worms profitable?
Yes, for an ounce of their eggs is worth more than their weight in gold.

Who first turned their attention to the raising of silk worms in Louisiana?
The early French settlers.

Where is the business most extensive?
In France and Italy.

How does the Louisiana silk worm compare with that of France and Italy?
It is larger, more valuable, and free from disease.

THE SILK WORM comes from China. The Chinese were the first people to engage in the manufacture of silk from the worms. A monk of the eleventh century, it is said, got a few worms from China. He obtained, also, some of the secrets regarding their culture.

CHAPTER VIII.

THE WILD BEASTS, GAME AND FISHES.

WILD BEASTS.

What wild beasts are to be found in Louisiana?

Several very large and fierce—such as bears, wolves, panthers, and wild cats.

Name some of the smaller animals.

Hares, rabbits, squirrels, opossums, muskrats, minks and raccoons.

How many varieties are there of squirrels?

Four.

Can you name them?

Grey, red, black, and flying squirrels.

What two animals are found near water-courses?

The beaver and the otter.

BIRDS.

What can you say of the feathered game of the State?

It is remarkably abundant.

What are the most famous, and the most highly prized?

Wild turkey, wild geese, brent, woodcock, partridge, prairie-quail, pheasant, paillenqueue, papabotte, cherook, *grostête* (big head), snipes, *grosbecks* (big beaks), robins, rails, blue and white cranes, flamingoes, and herons.

What are the best-known varieties of the duck ?

The canvas-back, the mallard, the blue-and-green wing, black, and teal.

THESE ARE THE BIG BIRDS. The woods are full of the little ones. They are full of the sweetest songsters—known only to the children of the city as sad prisoners in gilded cages. That King of Nature's Orchestra—the Mocking Bird—is at home, is free, there. Around him are scores of his feathered mates, whom he first maddens by his mimicry, and then charms by his music. There, too, are birds of the brightest colors, flitting airily from branch to branch, and making the green woods look gay and happy as they flash by.

What great naturalist has treated of the birds of America ?
JEAN JACQUES AUDUBON.

AUDUBON was born near New Orleans in 1780. When still a boy, he learned to love the little birds. When he grew to be a man he thought that he would write about them. He published a book. It was a great work. What struck the world with mingled wonder and admiration was to see that AUDUBON had given, in his book, an exact picture—in size, shape, and color of its feathers— of every bird, large and small, that sang, twittered, hopped and flew in the forests of Louisiana, or swam in its rivers and streams.

What has made Audubon immortal?
No man, before him, had ever succeeded so perfectly in bringing the birds, just as they are, out of the woods into a book.

AUDUBON'S GREAT WORK costs too much to be bought by everybody. It is found in most of the public libraries of the country ; and, now and then, in the larger private libraries.

FISHES.

Into how many classes may the fishes of Louisiana be divided?
Into salt-water and fresh-water fishes.

What are those known as salt-water fishes?

Those found in the Gulf of Mexico and the salt-water lakes.

Where are the fresh-water fishes found?

In the rivers, bayous and fresh water streams of the State.

Can you name the principal salt-water fishes?

Red fish, the sheephead, the Spanish mackerel, the croaker, flounder, sand-digger, black mullet, sometimes called "ground mullet," black drum, and trout.

What highly-prized fish is found among them?

The pompano.

THE POMPANO has a world-wide fame. Strangers visiting New Orleans do not like to leave the city without having tasted, at least once, this delicious fish. It comes in the spring, and is caught for a few weeks only. The first pompano in the market is eagerly sought after, and commands a high price.

What shell fish are also included in this division?

Several varieties of turtle, such as the green turtle, hawk-bill turtle, (so called from the shape of its bill) and the terrapin.

THE GREEN TURTLE is the most esteemed by the lovers of good eating. The green turtle soup and steaks are famous, everywhere.

What varieties can you name among the fresh-water fishes?

Buffalo, perch, sacalait, choupique, catfish, white cat, trout, bar, pike, and the soft shell turtle.

THE CAT FISH is that which is most common in Louisiana waters. It sometimes reaches a great size. Its meat is not over-delicate; but it makes good soup. The cat-fish is easily caught, as it is very greedy, and does more snapping than nibbling at a hook

Besides these, can you name some fishes that belong both to the salt and fresh water along the coast?

The gar-dolphin, shark and stingaree.

THESE WORTHLESS FISHES are the despair of fishermen. They chase away the good fish, and never get into the nets without breaking them. They are too fierce to be pleasant company; and their flesh is too rank and coarse to be pleasant eating.

THE END.